Letts

A-level
In a Week

Sociology

AQA

Year 1 / AS

**Andy Bennett
and
Scott Keifer**

CONTENTS

The Functionalist and New Right Perspectives on Education

Functionalism is a **consensus perspective** that believes society works like a human body with different parts working together for the smooth running of society as a whole. Functionalists call this the **organic analogy**. One of these interdependent parts is the education system, which functionalists believe serves a number of key functions for society.

Social Solidarity and Specialist Skills

Emile Durkheim (1913) was the founder of functionalism. He believed that for society to work effectively its members must share common beliefs and values. According to Durkheim the education system passes on these shared beliefs from one generation to another. This creates a sense of **social solidarity**; students learn skills for the future and develop a shared awareness of society's rules which allows them to interact with other people in the workplace.

Durkheim also believed that the education system teaches people **specialist skills** in order for them to play a role in the complex division of labour that is needed in modern industrial society. Each item that is produced in society requires the combined efforts of a number of individuals with different specialist skills.

EVALUATION POINT

School effectiveness is mainly measured around students' performance in core subjects like English and maths. This suggests that the education system may neglect to fully promote a wide range of specialist skills in an array of subject areas.

Meritocracy

Talcott Parsons (1961) stated that school acts as a form of secondary socialisation. He compared the education system to a bridge between home and work. At home a child is ascribed their status; it is simply given to them, for example, the 'son of the family' – they are judged by particularistic standards that only apply to them. In wider society people must work for their status, for example, 'business manager' – here they are judged by universalistic standards that apply to everyone. The education system, according to Parsons, teaches people to work for an **achieved status**, such as the one they will have to work for in their future roles. Alongside this, the system allows children to prepare to be judged by the universalistic standards of society.

Parsons believed the education system to be a **meritocracy**. This means a place where everyone has an equal chance of success. Individuals' rewards are the result of effort and ability.

EVALUATION POINT

Marxists disagree with Parsons; they believe that the education system does not provide equal opportunities for all students. Marxists suggest that the ruling class have a significant advantage in the education system.

Role Allocation

Kingsley Davis and Wilbert Moore (1945) believed that school sifts and sorts students into their future roles. The education system acts as a method of working out which people are more talented, or are more able to take more complex roles in society. Individuals' talents are identified through the education system. This is followed by **role allocation**, where people are allocated jobs that best suit their abilities. Peter Blau and Otis Duncan acknowledged that the modern economy relies on workers' skills in order to thrive; they described these skills as **'human capital'**.

The New Right

The **New Right** is a Conservative political view. They agree with the key principles of the functionalist view. However, the New Right believe that the education system is failing to provide these key functions effectively. In order to be successful, the New Right think that the education system should not be controlled by the state. The New Right favour **marketisation** of the education system. They feel that schools should compete against each other for customers (parents, who select the school for their child). Through competition, standards in schools would improve and in turn there would be an increase in the quality of education provided.

John Chubb and Terry Moe (1990) believed that the education system in the USA had failed, directly as a result of being run by the state. They believed that because of this, it has not allowed for equal opportunities for all students; it has also failed to provide the range of specialist skills needed for the wider economy. Chubb and Moe believed that the success of private schools, which are held accountable by paying customers (parents), highlights the failure of the state to provide a **meritocratic** education system.

The New Right believe that the state should still play two important roles in the education system. Firstly, it should facilitate the system in which schools compete against each other by providing Ofsted inspections and league tables. These can be used by parents to select the schools for their children. Secondly, in order to promote social solidarity and a sense of shared culture, the state should impose a set curriculum which every student should follow.

The New Right believes that a set curriculum should be imposed to promote social solidarity and a sense of shared culture.

SUMMARY

- Functionalism is a consensus perspective. The education system is just one of many interdependent parts needed for the smooth running of society as a whole.

- Durkheim believed the education system should provide social solidarity and equip individuals with specialist skills needed for society.

- Parsons believed that the education system is meritocratic and teaches students to work for their achieved status.

- Davis and Moore credited the education system as providing role allocation for future roles in wider society.

- The New Right agree with the roles that functionalists suggest the education system performs; they argue that the current system is failing due to state involvement.

- Marketisation must take place in order for schools to improve according to the New Right. Schools must compete against each other in order to be selected by parents for their children.

QUICK TEST

1. What is meant by the term 'organic analogy'?

2. Which term does Emile Durkheim use to describe the effect of a shared set of beliefs which are passed on from generation to generation by the education system?

3. What is meant by the 'marketisation' of the education system?

4. Davis and Moore believed the education system 'sifts and sorts' people into jobs. What term do they use for this key function?

5. What is a 'meritocratic' system?

6. Suggest two ways in which schools compete against each other.

7. What term did Blau and Duncan use to describe workers' skills that benefit society?

8. According to Parsons what type of status does the education system train individuals to obtain?

9. Which key issue do the New Right blame the failure of the education system on?

10. Which functionalist sociologist believes that the education system acts as a bridge between home and work?

PRACTICE QUESTIONS

Item A

Many sociologists believe that the education system acts as a vital interdependent part of society ensuring that all students have an equal chance to succeed and a role to play in wider society. They believe that regardless of social class, ethnicity or gender, every student has the opportunity to use their own efforts and ability to achieve.

Some sociologists disagree with this claim; they suggest that the education system fails to provide a fair chance for all. They believe that the ruling class have a significant advantage over others.

Question 1 (AS Level style): Applying material from Item A and your knowledge, evaluate the view that the education system creates an equal chance for all students to prepare for a role in wider society that reflects their ability. (20 marks) **Spend 30 minutes on your response.**

HINTS TO HELP YOU RESPOND

You will have about 30 minutes to respond to this type of question in an AS exam. Explain that the view is that of a functionalist. Introduce the core functionalist beliefs of meritocracy and role allocation. Use the evaluative points of Marxists to argue against the idea of meritocracy (use Bowles and Gintis from pages 8–9 to support this). Use Parsons to explain how all have a chance to achieve their status. Evaluate this using evidence that equal opportunities for success in education do not exist (you can select examples from class, gender or ethnic differences in achievement here). Make sure you are evaluating the view by criticising the functionalist argument throughout.

Question 2 (AS and A Level style): Outline three roles of the education system according to functionalist sociologists. (6 marks) **Spend 9 minutes on your response.**

HINTS TO HELP YOU RESPOND

Here you can select from a range of roles: social solidarity, specialist skills, role allocation, human capital, meritocracy and achieved status. You need to make sure that you explain each term (or role) including the key term. Start each point on a new line. Each point is worth 2 marks and should ideally be no more than two sentences. For example: 'Emile Durkheim believed that the education system provides social solidarity. It does this by transmitting shared ideas and beliefs from one generation to the next.'

The Marxist Perspective on Education

Marxism is a **conflict perspective** that sees society as based on a class divide. Karl Marx (1818–1883) believed there to be two classes in society: the **bourgeoisie** (capitalist or ruling class) who are smaller in numbers yet own the means of production (factories, land, etc.) and the **proletariat** (the working class) who own nothing except their own ability to work. This two class system causes **class conflict** as the working class are **exploited** by the capitalist class. They are forced to work under the pay and conditions that the capitalist class establish. This system of exploitation continues as the bourgeoisie also control the state. Marxists see the education system as key in maintaining the class divide.

Ideological State Apparatus

Louis Althusser (1971) focused on how the bourgeoisie control the state; this allows them to keep power over the proletariat. Althusser believed there to be two ways in which the bourgeoisie establish and maintain their power over the proletariat.

- The **repressive state apparatus** (RSA). This maintains the bourgeoisie's power by using force. It includes agencies such as the police, law courts and the army.
- The **ideological state apparatus** (ISA) establishes control over the ideas, beliefs and values of the proletariat. Along with the media and the family, among others, the education system serves as an ISA.

In order to work as an ISA the education system serves two key roles. It **reproduces class inequality** from one generation to the next, ensuring that children end up in the same social class as their parents. The education system also **legitimates class inequality** by causing individuals to believe that their own success is down to their ability and effort, not simply the result of the social class that they are born into.

EVALUATION POINT

Here you can use a number of functionalist arguments which show the fairness of the education system to argue against Althusser. Talcott Parsons' concept of meritocracy shows that all students have an equal chance of success regardless of their social class.

Obedience and the Correspondence Principle

Bowles and Gintis (1976) noted that, for capitalist society to work, the proletariat must be **obedient**, submissive and willing to work hard. They believed that the education system instils obedience in the working class so that they accept the need to work hard for little pay. Bowles and Gintis saw the education system's role as making the working class accept that social class inequality is inevitable. They saw the education system as having a 'hidden curriculum': by simply attending school, students learn lessons about the workings of the world, not just the knowledge gained in subject lessons.

In order to create an obedient workforce that is ready to serve capitalism, Bowles and Gintis looked at how the education system is highly similar to the world of work, preparing the working class for a life of obedient wage-slavery. They called this link the **correspondence principle**. There are a number of ways in which school mirrors work:

School	Work
Authority is in a hierarchy, e.g. pupils – teachers – assistant heads – deputy heads – head teacher.	Authority is in a hierarchy, e.g. workers – supervisors – managers – bosses.
There is competition which causes division between pupils, e.g. setting.	There is competition which causes division between workers, e.g. different pay levels.
Pupils have no real control over their education and they feel alienated (as though they are powerless) as a result.	Workers have no control over their production and in turn they feel alienated.
Rather than being satisfied by gaining knowledge, students are extrinsically rewarded with grades.	Rather than being rewarded by job satisfaction, workers are extrinsically rewarded by pay.

Bowles and Gintis discussed that the education system instils a set of ideas in people which make them unaware of the fact that they are being exploited. It creates a 'myth' that the individuals who gain high grades and rewards deserve them most as they are the most hard working and able. This concept is called the **'myth of meritocracy'**; this ensures that the proletariat accept their position in society and continue to work as **wage-slaves** for the bourgeoisie. Bowles and Gintis studied 237 high schools in New York and concluded that schools reward obedience over creativity. This creates an obedient workforce to serve the bourgeoisie.

EVALUATION POINT

Postmodernists suggest that this view of the education system is outdated and believe that class divisions in society are no longer relevant. They believe the system to now be much more diverse to reflect the changes in the jobs market, which means that people have to be trained in a wide range of skills. They believe that the education system, rather than serving to create inequality, creates a diverse workforce who think independently and do not simply do as they are told.

Learning to Labour

Paul Willis (1977) studied a group of 12 working class boys as they moved from school into the world of work. He found that rather than simply becoming 'obedient', like Bowles and Gintis would suggest, the boys developed an **anti-school subculture**, rejecting the school's values. Willis noted that, despite a lack of obedience, the boys still ended up in working class jobs. By going against the values of the school the boys caused their own failure, furthering their position as wage-slaves for the bourgeoisie.

EVALUATION POINT

Willis' study was on a very small scale; with only 12 boys involved it is certainly not representative. Feminist Angela McRobbie cited that Willis' study neglects to include any girls and therefore fails to represent the working class effectively. Willis' unstructured interviews and observations gathered qualitative data that is hard to quantify in order to portray trends.

Educational Policy and Marxism

Many educational policies have further created a class divide and highlighted the importance of the Marxist argument. Marketisation, introduced by the New Right in 1988, has impacted on the ability of the working class to be educated in the most effective schools (see pages 40–41 and 44–45 for more).

SUMMARY

- Marxism is a conflict perspective believing society to be made up of the bourgeoisie (ruling or capitalist class) and the proletariat (wage-slaves or working class). There is class conflict in this two class system as the proletariat are exploited by the bourgeoisie.

- Louis Althusser stated that the education system is an ideological state apparatus, controlling the beliefs, ideas and values of the working class in order for them to accept their exploited position in society. According the Althusser the education system reproduces and legitimates class inequality.

- The education system creates an obedient workforce, according to Bowles and Gintis. There are striking similarities between the schools and the workplace which reinforce this. This is called the correspondence principle.

- Individuals are controlled to believe that those who succeed do so due to their own hard work and ability, rather than simply as a result of the social class that they are born into. This is called the 'myth of meritocracy'.

- Paul Willis' study argued against the education system instilling obedience in all students. However, he found that even when working class students reject the values of the school system they still end up in working class jobs, reproducing class inequality.

- Alongside other educational policies, marketisation has further served to reinforce class inequality in the education system.

QUICK TEST

1. What do the bourgeoisie own?

2. According to Bowles and Gintis the education system tricks people into thinking that their hard work will be rewarded. What term did they use to describe this?

3. What is meant by the term 'correspondence principle'?

4. Name two ways in which the correspondence principle works.

5. In Paul Willis' study, what did the 12 boys form which meant that their values went against those of the school?

6. What policies were introduced in 1988 by the New Right, which further caused class inequality in the education system?

7. Which behaviour trait did Bowles and Gintis find schools rewarded?

8. According to Louis Althusser, what does the education system act as?

9. What are the two key roles that Louis Althusser stated the education system serves?

10. According to Marxists what do the proletariat own?

PRACTICE QUESTIONS

Item A

Marxist sociologists outline the notion that the education system plays a key role in causing a class divide in society. They believe that in order for capitalism to work, the ruling class need an obedient workforce that is willing to wage-slave in order to produce material goods for low pay and to accept their place below the bourgeoisie in society. Some Marxists believe that school mirrors the workplace causing working class students to prepare for a life of obedience; other Marxists would suggest that the education system causes the working class to reject school values and consequently fail in the education system and fall into working class roles.

Question 1 (A Level style): Applying material from Item A and your knowledge, evaluate the Marxist perspective on the education system. (30 marks) **Spend 45 minutes on your response.**

HINTS TO HELP YOU RESPOND

You need to look at each function that Marxists see the education system as serving and examine them clearly. Following each Marxist viewpoint add an evaluative criticism. Start by outlining the core beliefs of Marxism and its negative view of the education system. Move on to explain the views of Althusser and the system reproducing and legitimating class inequality; be sure to explain each of these terms well and further develop them using Bowles and Gintis and Paul Willis to add depth to your arguments. Aim to include a chain of reasoning in your response by planning your essay for at least 5 minutes before responding. Consider which points naturally support and argue against others, e.g. the myth of meritocracy serves to legitimise class inequality (here you are using Bowles and Gintis to support the works of Althusser).

Use Item A to help you, drawing on its points by looking for key hooks to discuss. Argue against the Marxist views you discuss by using the ideas of functionalists and ensure that you link these in effectively, e.g. use Talcott Parsons to argue against the myth of meritocracy; use social solidarity to argue against people being blindly obedient.

Question 2 (AS Level style): Outline and explain two roles that the education system plays according to Marxists. (10 marks) **Spend 15 minutes on your response.**

HINTS TO HELP YOU RESPOND

There are a number of roles that you can select here: the ideological state apparatus, creating an obedient workforce, mirroring work through the correspondence principle, forming anti-school subcultures among the working class to ensure they stay in working class roles, etc.

Aim to create two detailed paragraphs that follow the PEEL structure of Point, Evidence, Explain and Link. For example, you may select the ideological state apparatus as one role to discuss. Make your point by stating the system is an ideological state apparatus. Explain this with Louis Althusser and exactly what an ISA is, evidence this by discussing how the system acts to reproduce and legitimate class inequality in the education system and link to the question again by tying this to Marxism and the notion that by acting as an ISA the education system serves to keep the bourgeoisie in their dominant position over the proletariat.

Social Class Differences in Achievement: External Factors

Social class is measured in a number of different ways with most sociologists using the occupations of parents and their income to determine the social class of a child. As an example, working class parents will be in manual work or trades which are skilled, such as building, plumbing or driving machines. Middle class parents will have professional roles, often as office workers or business owners.

Statistically, children from middle class families outperform children from working class families in the education system. In schools, students will be allocated **free school meals** if their home income is below a certain level. Using this indicator is one way to measure the class gap in achievement. In state-funded schools in England in 2015, only 33·1% of students who received free school meals achieved 5 A*–C grades at GCSE, including English and maths, compared with 60·9% of all other pupils.

Many sociologists attribute this gap to factors outside the education system which they call **external factors** or 'home background factors'. These can be split into two types: cultural factors and material factors.

Cultural Deprivation

Children in different social classes are socialised differently, with the culture of a social class passing from one generation to the next. This means that children share the norms and values of the generation before them. As a result of this, many working class children find themselves without the norms, values and skills needed to perform well in the education system. Bourdieu (1984) called these skills and attitudes that put the middle class at an advantage **'cultural capital'**.

Throughout **primary socialisation**, which takes place in the home, children from middle class families are more likely to engage with activities that will encourage learning. They may learn to read with their parents at an early age. This puts them at an advantage when entering the education system.

Basil Bernstein (1975) examined the speech codes used by the different social class groups. He found that children from working class families are more likely to use a **restricted speech code**. This restricted code adopts a smaller vocabulary and uses simple sentences. Children from middle class families are more likely to use an **elaborated speech code**, which uses a much wider vocabulary and more complex sentence structures. The elaborated code is used by teachers, textbooks, exam papers, etc. As a result of this the middle class children are at an advantage in the education system.

EVALUATION POINT

The main reason why textbooks use an elaborated code is due to the fact that they cannot simply assume that the reader knows the content. They must explain content in detail, and elaborate code is the only type which fully addresses this issue.

Working Class Values

The shared norms and values of the working class include a number of key traits that are unique to the working class subculture. Barry Sugarman (1970) noted that the working class subculture is socialised to require **immediate gratification**. This means that students want their rewards as soon as they can get them. As a result of this, working class students lose sight of working hard through education to receive qualifications which later provide higher pay as a reward. Instead, working class students seek rewards by leaving education early to take jobs which reward them with pay now rather than in the future. Middle class students are at an advantage as they see the benefits of deferred gratification, allowing them to work through school for higher financial rewards in the world of work.

Some sociologists suggest that the working class subculture instils a **fatalistic attitude** in students. Working class students see that they will have little individual impact over their future positions and success, and in turn they may see little point in applying themselves fully in school. A lack of parental support has been cited to further cause this attitude. Douglas (1964) stated that working class parents show little interest in their child's schooling, which impacts on the child's own attitude towards education.

EVALUATION POINT

Cultural deprivation may be a factor from outside the education system and therefore cannot be solely blamed for underachievement of the working class, but it clearly has an impact on processes that occur within schools. For example, teacher labelling (see pages 16–17) may occur as a result of speech code. Cultural deprivation theory also fails to see the significant impact that material deprivation holds over educational success. The theory itself acts as a sweeping generalisation of the working class as the cause of their own underachievement, neglecting to look at the issues within the education system.

Material Deprivation

As children from working class families experience higher levels of poverty, they often experience **material deprivation** (a lack of the necessities needed for educational success). This deprivation can occur in a number of ways.

Halsey (1980) blamed a **lack of financial support** for working class students as the main cause of them leaving the education system earlier than middle class students.

Douglas (1964) blamed the **living conditions** of working class students for the underperformance in education. He pointed out that poor housing and overcrowding cause educational failure. For example, overcrowded housing impacts on achievement through the lack of personal space needed to focus on studies outside school. A **poor diet** can also have an impact, with a lack of the correct food leading to poor concentration in class and poor health which leads to school absences.

Opportunities within education are often expensive, with school trips, home tutoring, etc., placing students who can afford these at an advantage. Acceptance from peers in school can also have an impact on a student's performance, with clothing needed to 'fit in' with others often being unaffordable for working class families.

Bourdieu (1984) stated that the **economic capital** that middle class families have places their children at a significant advantage over the working class. Taking a Marxist approach Bourdieu noted the wealth that is reproduced within middle class families is a significant cause of an achievement gap between the social classes, alongside the cultural capital of the middle class.

EVALUATION POINT

There are still, and will always be, working class students who achieve highly in the education system despite experiencing material deprivation. It can be argued that material deprivation holds less significance than the internal factors which cause working class underachievement (see pages 16–17).

SUMMARY

- Statistics show that children from middle class families outperform those from working class families in the education system.

- Factors outside the education system, known as 'external factors', influence this class gap in achievement.

- Cultural deprivation impacts on the working class in a number of ways, from use of language to attitudes that the working class subculture share.

- Basil Bernstein noted that the working class use a restricted speech code, which proves to be a barrier when accessing teachers and textbooks, which use an elaborated speech code.

- Working class children often favour immediate gratification, meaning that they are eager to leave the education system to start earning money.

- A fatalistic attitude is often shared by working class children, which impacts on the effort that they are willing to put into their schooling.

- Due to poverty, many working class students are materially deprived, which impacts on their living conditions and diet.

- Bourdieu believed economic and cultural capital to be a significant advantage to middle class students.

QUICK TEST

1. What do schools and sociologists use as an indicator of social class?

2. What is meant by the term 'cultural capital'?

3. Which key term is used to describe a lack of physical necessities needed for educational success?

4. Which sociologist stated that a lack of financial support restricts the working class from staying in education?

5. According to Basil Bernstein, what type of speech code do middle class students use, and why does this place them at an advantage in education?

6. Which term describes the view that there is little point in trying in education as the working class will not be able to change their position?

7. What is meant by the term 'immediate gratification'?

8. What term did Bourdieu use for the wealth that the middle class have, giving them an advantage in education?

9. In 2015, what percentage of students eligible for free school meals in state-funded schools achieved 5 A*–C grades at GCSE including English and maths?

10. How might a poor diet impact on a student's achievement?

PRACTICE QUESTIONS

Question 1 (AS Level style): Outline and explain two sociological explanations as to why working class students do not perform as highly as middle class students in the education system. (10 marks) **Spend 15 minutes on your response.**

HINTS TO HELP YOU RESPOND

Remember to always read the question carefully, looking for exactly what your response must entail. Here you are being asked to 'explain' as well as 'outline' two explanations. You can select from any of the factors mentioned in this topic: primary socialisation, speech codes, immediate gratification, fatalistic attitudes, material deprivation, etc. (and also from the internal factors on pages 16–17). The best way to approach this is with two detailed PEEL paragraphs (point, evidence, explain and link to the question).

For example: 'Many working class students share similar attitudes and values which place them at a disadvantage in the education system, with a lack of support from their parents who may not value the education system. As a result of this, working class students may favour immediate gratification, that is, they will seek rewards sooner rather than later. This means that working class students are often reluctant to wait to the end of the education system for the reward of significant qualifications. They are more likely to leave the education system early in order to seek employment for wages as soon as possible. This will impact on their success as they will not be aiming for higher qualifications, resulting in working class students achieving lower grades than middle class students.'

Question 2 (AS and A Level style): Outline three reasons why material deprivation may impact on a working class student's achievement in school. (6 marks) **Spend 9 minutes on your response.**

HINTS TO HELP YOU RESPOND

This question is simply asking you to 'outline' each reason. You can select from any of the material deprivation examples, e.g. lack of financial support, overcrowded living conditions, poor diet. Start each point on a new line and keep your responses short and precise. For example: 'Material deprivation may include a poor diet, which will impact on working class students as they may not be able to concentrate in class and they are more likely to experience poor health causing them to be absent from school.'

Social Class Differences in Achievement: Internal Factors

Social class differences in achievement are often considered to be a result of the education system itself and the way in which it operates. Factors that exist within the school system are known as **internal factors** or 'school processes'. These include concerns about the way in which working class students are treated in the education system and the groups that they may form as a response.

Labelling

To apply a label to someone is simply to attach a meaning or definition to them. For example, 'lazy' or 'scruffy'. Howard Becker (1961) conducted 60 interviews with high school teachers in Chicago. He found that teachers had a definite view of what they saw to be the **'ideal pupil'**. Students' conduct, work rate and appearance were all factors that were taken into account when teachers made judgements about students. Students from middle class backgrounds were more likely to be **labelled** as the 'ideal pupil'. Working class students were more likely to be labelled negatively by teachers.

The Self-Fulfilling Prophecy

As a direct result of labelling, a **self-fulfilling prophecy** may occur. This is simply when a label is applied to a child, the child internalises that label and eventually this causes the label to become true. For example, if a child is labelled as someone who is likely to fail, this is likely to result in them failing their exams.

Rosenthal and Jacobson (1968) studied the impact of the 'self-fulfilling prophecy' on a group of students. They conducted a field experiment at a primary school in America. Students at the primary school were given a standard IQ test and a small group were then selected completely at random from the results. Teachers at the school were informed that these students were able to make significant progress. After returning to the school to administer the IQ test again, Rosenthal and Jacobson found that the IQ level of the students identified as able to make significant progress had risen in comparison to the IQ levels of the other students.

Not all working class students who are negatively labelled will fail as a result. Some students may actively challenge and reject their negative labels, working towards success. Labelling theory can be considered too deterministic; it cannot seem possible to consider that all working class students are negatively labelled by teachers and each of these labels cannot result in a self-fulfilling prophecy. Labelling may, however, occur as a result of the teacher's view of external factors, such as a student using a restricted language code. Many internal factors may be a direct result of an external factor. Teachers may judge a pupil as academically weak, labelling them as a result of their restricted use of language.

Setting and Streaming

Labelling of students is rooted in the practices of schools. By placing students in sets and streams based on their perceived ability, schools actively label students, with working class pupils being placed in the lower sets. Colin Lacey (1970) stated that **streaming** is **'differentiation'**, a way of sorting students into groups in order to be taught differently. This differentiation often creates a self-fulfilling prophecy, with the IQ of students in lower sets or streams falling over time.

Pro- and Anti-school Subcultures

When placed in different sets and streams, and as a response to labelling, students often fall into subcultures that reflect their values towards school. For example, students in higher sets may become members of a **pro-school subculture**. Within a pro-school subculture students are likely to take part in more school activities, celebrate the success of their peers and take part in activities which promote learning. As a result of teacher labelling the students in pro-school subcultures are more likely to be middle class and consequently achieve more than students outside this subculture.

Working class students are more likely to be labelled negatively and therefore find themselves in an **anti-school subculture**. Students in anti-school subcultures reject the values of school and often find themselves in conflict with teachers. Truancy and a poor standard of uniform are likely among anti-school subcultures.

Working Class Identity and its Impact in School

The working class share norms and values and as a result they have a shared thought process. This is called their 'habitus'. The middle class **'habitus'** (shared thought process) is seen as superior in school and as a result the working class are isolated and devalued. By following the middle class habitus, students gain symbolic capital (the status needed to do well in education). This means that working class students lack this **symbolic capital**. Schools commit **symbolic violence** towards the working class by denying them the opportunity to gain symbolic capital. Schools reject working class accents, clothing, hobbies and interests, further isolating working class students.

According to Archer (2010) working class students often create their own class identities in order to gain status among their peers, as they are denied the symbolic capital of the middle class. One way in which they may do this is by affiliating with a brand, for example through developing **'Nike identities'** by wearing branded goods. This causes further conflict with the middle class habitus. Archer stated that working class students may have to change who they are to 'fit in' and succeed. Archer called this **'losing yourself'**.

Impact of Policy

Many sociologists argue that educational policies have further caused these internal factors to escalate the class gap in achievement. For example, in 1965 when all students were to attend **comprehensive schools**, setting and streaming increased across schools.

SUMMARY

- Many sociologists see factors inside the education system (internal factors) as causes for the achievement gap between middle class and working class students.
- Howard Becker stated that teachers label students based on how closely they fit their image of the 'ideal pupil'.
- Working class students are negatively labelled by teachers; this often leads to a self-fulfilling prophecy, with teachers' predictions becoming true.
- Schools actively label groups of students by streaming and setting them. This differentiation often means that working class students are taught differently.
- Middle class students in top streams are likely to form pro-school subcultures, furthering their success in the education system. Working class students in lower sets are likely to become members of an anti-school subculture.
- The middle class habitus is seen as superior in schools and, as a result of this, working class students are denied the symbolic capital for success in education that middle class students have.
- Schools commit acts of symbolic violence towards the working class, rejecting their habitus.
- Comprehensive educational policies have further established patterns of setting and streaming which add to the class gap in achievement.

QUICK TEST

1. Which sociologist looked into teachers' labelling of students based on how closely they fit the image of the 'ideal pupil'?

2. What did Colin Lacey call streaming, which results in working class students being taught lesser content?

3. What did Archer mean by 'Nike identities'?

4. Which key term is used for a thought process shared by a social class?

5. According to Archer, what might working class students have to do in order to 'fit in'?

6. What is the term given to the process which may occur following the labelling of a student?

7. What do middle class students gain as a result of the education system favouring their habitus?

8. Which sociologists studied the impact of the 'self-fulfilling prophecy' by use of IQ testing?

9. Note three traits of the anti-school subculture.

10. Give one example of symbolic violence against the working class habitus.

PRACTICE QUESTIONS

Item A

There is statistical evidence to suggest that the working class are at a significant disadvantage in the education system, with working class students being treated differently to the middle class by teachers and forming subcultures that reject school values as a result. Many sociologists believe factors that take place within schools are the main cause of a gap in achievement between social classes; others suggest that factors outside the education system are predominantly to blame.

Question 1 (AS Level style): Applying material from Item A, evaluate the view that underachievement among working class students is the result of school processes. (20 marks) **Spend 30 minutes on your response.**

HINTS TO HELP YOU RESPOND

In this response you are asked to 'evaluate'. This means looking at the advantages and disadvantages of the argument. You will note that the core debate within your essay here is about whether or not internal factors are to blame for the class gap in achievement, as the question mentions 'school processes'. You will evaluate these with external factors. Your response must naturally link between points to form a chain of reasoning. For example, discuss labelling and Howard Becker (use the item here and mention the part which states that working class students are treated differently), then add an external factor which might impact upon labelling. An example of this would be to suggest that teachers label students due to the language that they use; here you will use Bernstein and restricted language codes. Between your points use connectives which show you are evaluating, such as 'in contrast to this' or 'supporting this theory'. You could conclude that underachievement among working class students is a result of both internal and external factors.

Item B

Working class students often experience a negative attitude towards the ways in which they strive to establish their own identity and values. Some sociologists suggest that this is due to the education system favouring the thought processes and values of the middle class. There are a number of ways in which working class students might respond to this. They may seek to make themselves stand out, or simply change who they are by acting in a different way to fit in with their peers.

Question 2 (A Level style): Applying material from Item B, analyse two responses by working class students to negative attitudes towards their habitus. (10 marks) **Spend 15 minutes on your response.**

HINTS TO HELP YOU RESPOND

You must use two points from the item; think carefully about where you will get your two points from. You will note that the item mentions 'standing out', which could be linked to Nike identities. The item also discusses 'simply changing', which could reflect Archer's 'losing yourself'. In analysing, discuss each point and explain it, then question it. For example, you may discuss 'Nike identities' as a way to gain status in the working class habitus, then question this by noting that not all working class students do this. Here you can link into your next point about 'losing yourself'.

Gender Differences in Achievement: External Factors

The Patterns

Girls have achieved better results in early years education from the inception of 'Education for All'. More recently girls do better than boys across all key stages. At GCSE girls outperform boys in all subjects. In many subjects the margin of A*–C achievement is much better for girls. Maths is the only subject where the gender gap is narrower; in science the gap is narrower than the significant differences found in English. At A level girls outperform boys in terms of A–B grades but do not get as many A* grades. A gap exists at undergraduate degree level. Women outperform men by 5 percentage points when it comes to attaining a first class or upper second class honours degree. Haralambos and Holborn have shown that the boys have been narrowing the gap in recent years but this contradicts some interpretations that show both genders improving with the gap remaining constant between boys and girls.

Employment Patterns

Women have broken through the **glass ceiling** that was said to exist in the past. This was a transparent but very real barrier to women making progress to better paid jobs with greater responsibility, such as managerial or professional level careers. The Sex Discrimination Act 1975 and the Equal Pay Act 1970 were encouragements to women to seek roles outside being housewives and mothers. Role models appeared within society to encourage girls to shift their aspirations and the laws obviously reinforced this aspirational shift. Although a pay gap exists between men and women it has been halved to 15% since the passing of the Sex Discrimination Act (2013 report). The growth in the service sector in recent years has also contributed to more than two-thirds of women being in employment.

Feminist Ideas

The changes in the law mentioned above were encouraged by the activism of **feminist movements**. Traditional attitudes saw women as mothers, housewives and under the authority of men. These attitudes became characterised as stereotypes and harmful to the opportunities of women in a changing world. The lasting legacy of success has been greater equality between the sexes supported by changes in the law. These changes created the conditions for more assured attitudes within women from which grew generations who sought careers on an equal footing with men.

EVALUATION POINT

There is evidence from Angela McRobbie's study of images presented in girls' magazines of what roles they should be aiming to fill in adulthood that support the shifts described above. In the 1970s girls were advised on how not to be 'left on the shelf' while contemporary images show distinct career professionals as role models for girls. It must be cautioned that gender in and of itself is not the only factor determining differences in educational success. Some commentators advise that focusing on failing boys ignores a group of girls that are failing: the common factor here is economically disadvantaged working class children.

Changing Family Patterns

With increasing rates of divorce and the consequent increased numbers of female-headed lone-parent households it has been suggested that girls within these families have, from their lived experience, learnt not to be dependent on the traditional male breadwinner to support them. They have seen their own mothers as role models achieving success in work. Or they have experienced the hardships of the single income household. In each case they have been motivated to achieve independent success, a career for themselves and well-paid employment. In any of these scenarios better qualifications improve the independence and career prospects of girls.

Boys too come from single-parent households and should be motivated to succeed for the same reasons; perhaps it is a combination of factors that explains the higher achievement of girls in education. Many sociologists would emphasise the internal factors discussed in the next topic.

Aspirational Motivation

O'Connor supported the conclusions outlined above. Priorities for key stage 4 and 5 pupils were careers, not marriage. This builds on earlier studies conducted through interviews by Sue Sharpe on the shift in attitudes from careers being seen as unattractive and unfeminine in the 1970s to the independent, career minded individuals that exist today. The evidence for this attitudinal shift is further supported by Carol Fuller's study that found educational attainment to be key to individual identity. This supports Helen Wilkinson's ideas of a **genderquake** as girls' attitudes to work and their career aspirations and the family have been radically reshaped in recent years. The increased focus on the individual over obligations to family members, coupled with the belief in the meritocratic educational system, encouraged girls to aim for careers that required degree level qualifications. Burns and Bracey (2001) found that girls are much more motivated and harder working. Boys are less motivated because they have unrealistic career plans, according to Becky Francis (2000), based on careers in sport that require few academic qualifications.

Social class complicates this rather neat picture of girls' success and boys' relative failure. Where good job opportunities are scarce ambitions become stunted and the more stereotypical gender roles persist. Diane Reay found that marriage and motherhood provided a status to a girl that was attainable.

Gender-Role Socialisation

Boys, Edwards and David found, are socialised to behaviours outside school that cause disruption in school, such as not being required to be as quiet as girls in the home. At home girls are socialised to stillness and to reading. This means they are better at sitting still in the classroom for long periods. Other masculine traits that disrupt learning are socialised in and out of school. So boys relate by doing, girls by talking. Thus girls are better at paired or group activities. Boys do not value academic achievement as it is seen as feminine whereas sporting success is seen as masculine.

It is clear that no single point within this topic is solely to blame for patterns in gender achievement. A range of external and internal factors must be examined to fully understand the wider picture. Internal factors must be taken into account such as teacher attention, increased numbers of positive role models for girls in secondary education and the lack of male role models for boys in primary education.

SUMMARY

- Girls outperform boys at all levels of education; the gap has not grown and both genders have improved their attainment levels since the late 1980s.

- The glass ceiling has been broken providing an example for girls to aspire to higher paid jobs.

- The Sex Discrimination Act 1975 and the Equal Pay Act 1970 have obligated society to shift to a more equal, democratic and fair attitude toward women in employment.

- Feminist ideas have filtered through society changing for ever girls' attitudes towards their own roles within society. This has been described as a genderquake.

- Gender-role socialisation still exerts a negative influence on boys, preventing them from working hard in school.

QUICK TEST

1. Which acts of parliament encouraged women to seek out employment opportunities?

2. Give two ways in which changing family patterns encouraged girls to be more career minded.

3. Which sociologist described girls being influenced by media that encouraged them to fear being unwed or 'left on the shelf' and so reading materials that reinforced traditional gender-role stereotypes?

4. Which attitudinal shift did the sociologist Carol Fuller pinpoint as crucial to the gender gap in educational achievement?

5. What does the term 'genderquake' mean?

6. What did the sociologist Francis say was the key to understanding boys' lack of motivation towards academic success?

7. What did Diane Reay believe working class girls, who failed in comparison to other social groups, get from marriage and motherhood?

8. Give two ways in which boys' gender-role socialisation outside school prevents them from gaining success in school.

9. Why do boys not value academic success?

10. What did Burns and Bracey state about girls' attitudes to school?

PRACTICE QUESTIONS

Item A

Baby girls are talked to by their mothers more frequently than baby boys. Some sociologists see this as an explanation of the higher attainment of girls in education as girls acquire better language skills than boys. Girls are motivated in school and able to sit and study as this compliant attitude is encouraged in the home from an early age. Changes in family structure, the changes in the jobs available and the aspirations of girls have also played significant parts in improved results of girls in education.

Question 1 (A Level style): Applying material from Item A, analyse two external factors that create gender differences in educational achievement. (10 marks) **Spend 15 minutes on your response.**

HINTS TO HELP YOU RESPOND

Here you must discuss two factors in detail and suggest weaknesses, strengths or counterpoints to the 'factors' you explain. You must link your two factors to points from the item. You will see gender-role socialisation as one point of focus. There is evidence that shows boys are hampered in school by the socialisation that occurs within families. Engage the question directly from the start. You need to make sure that you fully explain how each factor leads to differences in educational attainment. For example: 'Women in work playing the major breadwinner role in lone-parent households provides girls with a new type of role model to aspire to. This leads to girls seeing careers as essential to their own independent futures as men cannot be necessarily relied on to provide for a family as divorce or desertion do happen. As a result of this many female students from lone-parent families should be expected to achieve highly.' Try to include detail in your paragraphs and follow the PEEL structure (point, evidence, explain and link back to the question). Use contrasting perspectives and evidence for the evaluation to reach the highest mark possible.

Question 2 (AS Level style): Outline three ways in which gender-role socialisation may cause differences in gender achievement in the education system. (6 marks) **Spend 9 minutes on your response.**

HINTS TO HELP YOU RESPOND

Your response here will be quite short. For each 'way' start a new line to show the examiner that you are outlining another point. You could discuss a range of gender-role socialisation factors here: boys' socialisation in the home compared to girls', changed family structure, aspirations of girls lifted, the genderquake, etc. Outlining your responses can be just two sentences each. For example: 'Many boys do less well than girls as they are socialised to do rather than to talk and read. This means that they do not do well in an environment where talking, listening and reading are of benefit in achieving educational success.'

Gender Differences in Achievement: Internal Factors

The Feminisation of Education – Girls Outperforming Boys

A number of internal factors have been used to explain the overall pattern of girls outperforming boys in education. Greater numbers of female teachers within the education system provide positive role models, reinforcing girls' attitudes that education can bring real benefits for women.

From the late 1980s deliberate steps were taken to make schools more girl-friendly. Sociological research had revealed an environment in the 1970s that favoured boys. The research by feminist sociologists followed on from the wider concerns to promote equality of opportunity throughout society. Stanworth (1990) found that boys were given more attention and that teachers had higher expectations of them. Spender (1983) claimed that girls' work was judged more harshly than boys'. Also, girls' questioning attitudes were discouraged as not being lady-like but boys' attitudes when challenging teachers were respected. Weiner (1995) argued that schools have been more forceful in challenging sexist attitudes since the 1980s and these earlier studies have been influential in showing boy-bias operating within the education system so that it can be reduced or removed.

Educational materials have also changed because of the studies of Spender and Stanworth. Gender stereotypes within these materials have been removed and positive images of a diverse range of roles have been presented to girls.

EVALUATION POINT

Myhill suggested that girls' success stems from their socialisation as compliant and conformist learners; these passive attributes hamper their attainment when they embark on professional careers. Schools are still patriarchal, argued Coffey and Delamont (2000), run in the main by males with the emphasis on regulation, masculine authoritarianism and with competition and hierarchy reflecting the wider sexism of male dominated society. Swann's (1998) research into the way that boys and girls interact in the classroom led him to suggest that teachers had the expectation that girls are cooperative, thus they valued their contributions and this raised their self-esteem. Boys talked over others in group work instead of taking turns, as the girls did, to listen and contribute. Boys felt that their contributions were met with disapproval from the teacher. Becky Francis found that the teachers had lower expectations of boys as they were seen to break the rules more often by calling out and being too dominant in discussions.

According to Mitsos and Browne (1998) the organisational qualities of girls and their conscientious approach to drafting and redrafting school coursework are significant factors in the better performance of girls compared to boys. Their presentation and ability to meet deadlines have enhanced their results since the introduction of GCSEs and coursework in 1988. Stephen Gorard's (2005) analysis of examination results supported these findings, that is, that boys are not failing but that the different assessment methods favour girls.

Marketisation

Girls have become more highly valued since competition between schools has been introduced. Roger Slee (1998) argued that boys are less likely to be recruited by the top performing schools because they are more likely to have behavioural problems. Exclusions among boys are four times that of girls. With league tables measuring school performance these boys are seen as **'liability students'**, potential barriers to a school rising up the league table. Conversely high achieving girls are sought after by the high performing schools in what becomes a **self-fulfilling prophecy** – boys go to bad schools and do badly, girls go to good schools and do better.

Subject Choices and Gender

- Boys more often choose maths and science, whereas girls choose languages or sociology, not physics, at A level.
- **Gender routes** exist even within a subject area like design and technology; girls choose food technology, boys choose resistant materials.
- Vocational courses show the same **gender bias**; only 1 in 100 students choosing childcare apprenticeships is a boy.
- **Gender-role socialisation** shapes gender identity from an early age. Fiona Norman and Ann Oakley have both commented on this early persuasion to specific gender stereotypes.
- **Gender domains** are the tasks regarded by boys and girls as specifically relevant to their gender identities. So from early on they regard certain tasks as masculine or feminine activities based on the expectations of adults. Naima Browne and Carol Ross used this concept to explain the gender divide in the popularity of subjects among girls and boys.
- Diana Leonard's research on **single-sex schools** found that less gender bias of subject choices existed in both all boy and all girl schools.
- The **gendered-subject images** may be stronger in mixed schools, where it is found that boys dominate apparatus, science teachers are often men and less group work (which girls enjoy) is practised.
- **Peer pressure** exerts tremendous influence on choices of subject; female students may be called 'butch' or 'lesbian' for selecting sports subjects which are outside the gender domain and go against traditional gender stereotypes.

EVALUATION POINT

Feminists argue that schools still promote patriarchal ideologies through gendered subject choices. The fact that these gendered choices exist is evidence of the promotion of gender stereotypes being reinforced by teacher behaviours, expectations and reinforcements.

Working Class Girls and Peer Pressure

Archer (2010) found that working class girls regulated each other's behaviour in a manner that clashed with ideas of what an 'ideal' school pupil should look like. Working class girls were popular with their peers if they adopted **hyper-sexualised feminine identities**. This meant investing in a certain look, wearing make-up in a specific manner to avoid labels such as 'tramp'. Currie found that shaming by negative labelling was used by girls to police the identity of girls so they would conform to a particular view of feminine sexual identity. Student behaviour was being encouraged by peer groups that caused clashes with the dominant school culture. This clash reinforced a **culture clash** between the home life of working class children and school culture when compared to the complementary cultures of the middle class home and school life. The values of the middle class home seem to extend into the education system and this means fewer problems adjusting to school expectations as they mirror expectations at home.

EVALUATION POINT

More especially male pupils who adopt the school's ideal pupil image may be labelled as 'boffins' but they resist the labelling by labelling the labellers as 'chavs'.

SUMMARY

- Female teachers are role models showing a path to successful professional careers for girls.

- Schools deliberately changed their attitudes towards teaching girls after studies revealed that girls were not treated fairly in school.

- Gender stereotypes within educational materials have been removed and the changed curriculum of the 1980s suited girls' abilities.

- Myhill suggested that girls' success stems from their socialisation as compliant and conformist learners.

- Marketisation policies have helped girls but hampered boys as good schools are more likely to reject boys as liability students and seek to attract the smart girls.

- Gender-role socialisation, gender domains and gender routes mean subject choices remain gendered and support traditional stereotypical expectations.

- Peer pressure can have a negative impact on girls' attainment.

QUICK TEST

1. Which two feminist sociologists discovered evidence of boy-bias in schools in the late 1970s and 1980s?

2. What did the findings of Coffey and Delamont suggest about schools today?

3. Why did Becky Francis say that teachers had lower expectations of boys?

4. Stephen Gorard found that boys were not failing compared to girls. What was his reason for stating this?

5. What are 'liability students'?

6. What are 'gender domains'?

7. How do working class girls try to gain status and acceptance among their peers?

8. How do girls police each other's identity in school?

9. What is meant by a 'culture clash'?

10. Why are some girls called 'butch' for wanting to do sport?

PRACTICE QUESTIONS

Item A
Patterns in achievement of boys and girls highlight the fact that many girls outperform boys in the education system. Some female students may suffer from peer pressure or teacher expectations of gender-role stereotypes. In recent years there have been changes within education that have been seen to favour girls and encouraged them to overtake boys. However, some students still face the peer pressure to conform to idealised feminine identities that do not fit into the ideal pupil image of schools.

Question 1 (A Level style): Applying material from Item A and your knowledge, evaluate the view that girls outperforming boys is due to processes within schools. (30 marks) **Spend 45 minutes on your response.**

HINTS TO HELP YOU RESPOND
Here you need to examine the internal factors that cause girls to do better than boys. Be precise in your explanation, ensuring that you use sociologists to support your key arguments of gender domains, curriculum changes and gender-role socialisation. Your response must show a clear thought pattern; create a 5 minute plan before starting your response, and consider which evaluative points fit where. In evaluating internal factors you will need to use external factors. For example, when you explain the shift from a boy-bias in schools, you can use ideas from the external factors on pages 20–21 to show how attitudes in schools are linked to changed ideas of gender roles more widely. Develop the points from the item and let the examiner know you are doing this by using terms such as: 'in Item A…' or 'the item suggests…' It will be difficult to be conclusive in stating that girls outperforming boys is simply a result of internal factors. You can conclude that all factors must be taken into account.

Question 2 (AS Level style): Define the term 'gender domains'. (2 marks) **Spend no more than 3 minutes on your response.**

HINTS TO HELP YOU RESPOND
With a 2 mark question, your response must be short and precise. By defining a term, state what the term is without using any words from the term itself. For example: 'Gender domains are the areas that men and women see as specifically relevant to their own personal identity as men and women, and are shaped from an early age.' If you struggle with the definitions use examples to illustrate your meaning – women cook and clean in the kitchen while men repair and mend in the garage. An example alone will not gain the full marks.

Question 3 (AS Level style): Using one example, briefly explain how gender-bias occurs in the education system. (2 marks) **Spend no more than 3 minutes on your response.**

HINTS TO HELP YOU RESPOND
Again, here, you will need to be short and precise with your response. Give an example of gender-bias and explain how it leads to bias. For example: 'Marketisation policies put in place by the New Right government in 1988 mean that schools can be selective over which students they accept. Schools have the ability to exclude boys, forcing them to attend poorer performing schools with lower chance of success. This is institutionally sexist as well as gender-biased as it places male students at a disadvantage.'

Gender and Achievement: Boys' Achievement and Social Class

Boys today are gaining better results than they did in the past. Both genders have improved markedly in the numbers achieving five A*–C grades in recent years. For Tracy McVeigh (2001) boys' and girls' achievements have more similarities than differences. For some sociologists the focus on gender differences ignores the complex relationships of class, gender and ethnicity. Jessica Ringrose has referred to the **moral panic** surrounding boys' perceived underachievement as harmful because the overreaction creates negative consequences as government policies seek to tackle the over-exaggerated threat of failing working class boys. These boys are portrayed as dangerous to social stability as they will become part of the **underclass** that is long-term unemployed and a drain on society's resources. Ringrose argued that this approach is wrong and avoids dealing with issues of ethnic and social disadvantage. The moral panic approach also blames girls for boys' perceived failure and draws attention away from a range of continuing problems for girls in education: sexual harassment, bullying, gendered subject choices, identity and mental health issues.

Peer Labelling and Laddish Culture

Boys reject the school culture because to accept the responsibilities of the ideal student would erode their own masculine gender identities, which for working class boys is based on the idea that 'men do manual work, men do not do reading and writing', as these tasks are **effeminate**, not manly. Negative labels like 'swot', 'geek' and a host of other derogatory homophobic labels marginalise boys who do conform to the ideal student type. This behaviour is part of what Debbie Epstein (1998) described as **laddish culture**. Francis has noted the increase of laddish culture as women are employed in wider numbers of careers that men thought were their preserve. Francis noted the behaviour is a kind of defence mechanism for masculine identity as it is threatened by feminisation.

EVALUATION POINT

Research by Hollingworth and Williams (2009) has shown that school subcultures are complex and that anti-school cultures, as described in the research from the 1970s, exist but are often identified as 'chav' rather than laddish culture. To see social class as the only basis for the development of anti-school culture is too simplistic. Issues of personal identity and sexuality must be considered when studying resistance to school authority or academic achievement.

Traditional Jobs for the Boys in Decline

One popular explanation of the demotivation of boys in education is the decline in traditional working men's jobs in heavy industry, e.g. ship building and manufacturing. Globalisation has resulted in this type of work moving abroad for economic reasons. With no prospect of a job the self-esteem of boys is damaged, as they see no future employment prospects and so give up on academic success. Mitsos and Browne have described this as an **'identity crisis'** as young men lose hope of fulfilling their role within society.

EVALUATION POINT

It can be argued that these jobs did not require academic qualifications. The jobs were low-skilled manual work. If this is true then the impact should be the reverse, with boys from this social class trying harder to gain qualifications for different areas of employment. However, the issues of self-esteem in a transitioning world economy affecting male identity do make for a persuasive point here.

Literacy and Language Skills

The **Department for Children, Schools and Families** (2007–2010, now replaced by the Department for Education) identified the poor literacy and language skills of boys as a cause of the gender gap in achievement. Boys' leisure activities did not build language skills because they were out playing football. Angela McRobbie identified girls as having a **bedroom culture**. This contributes positively to their education because here they chat and read in the bedroom. This improves their communication skills. These skills are highly valued in education. The physical pursuits of boys do not make such a positive contribution to schooling. In fact, it creates active and competitive boys where education values compliance and conformity. Literacy levels are also affected by reading being seen as a feminine activity. This stems from the mother being the parent that reads most with the children and so boys link reading to qualities that females possess. This is why many government strategies have tried to encourage male role models within their policy initiatives, e.g. The Reading Champions Scheme and The Dads and Sons campaign. Both encouraged fathers to take an active role in reading with their sons and become positive educational role models for boys.

EVALUATION POINT

Literacy levels cannot be analysed without taking anti-school subcultures into account. If an identity is rooted firmly in a rejection of the school image of an ideal pupil it can be too simplistic to identify a single strategy for improving attainment of a gender without taking the complex nature of **subcultures** into account. Subcultures are groups within society who share aspects of identity with each other: clothing, styles, musical tastes, attitudes to authority, language, etc. They will share aspects of the wider culture of society but have distinct sets of values themselves. The point here is that no single strategy can hope to achieve success for all; strategies must be tailored to different subcultures.

Gender-Bias in Education

Tony Sewell has argued that schools have challenged the patriarchal ideas that prevented girls from reaching their full potential. However, education is now failing boys because the curriculum is biased in favour of the skills that girls have. Boys' skills, their qualities as leaders and their competitiveness are not catered for by the requirements of coursework. Sewell supported the more recent emphasis on final year examinations and the abandonment of coursework requirements.

Primary schools have been targeted as a source of boys' underachievement. Specifically the lack of **male role models** within the teaching profession has led to a decline in boys' good behaviour. Male teachers are regarded as better able to keep disciplinary levels high enough for good learning to take place. YouGov found that almost half of boys thought that a male teacher made them behave better. This is important when the number of female-headed lone-parent households stands at 1·5 million. Importantly, more than a third of 8–11 year old boys will never have a male teacher.

EVALUATION POINT

Malcolm Haase and Barbara Read rejected the idea that schools have become feminised. Read found that a male **disciplinarian discourse** dominated in primary schools. It does not matter that the teachers are female as the structures and discipline employed are masculine. Men have a much greater chance of being heads of schools or in leadership positions so continuing the masculine disciplinarian discourse of shouting, sarcasm and visible condemnation of poor behaviour.

SUMMARY

- Many sociologists see boys' underachievement as a moral panic that ignores the similarities between the achievements of boys and girls.
- A laddish culture has been blamed for working class boys' rejection of the feminine qualities that are necessary for success in education.
- Globalisation has resulted in a decline in jobs in the manual sector of employment resulting in boys losing the motivation to do well as no job awaits them afterwards.
- Literacy and language skills are lacking in boys from an early age as they see these as feminine qualities and reject them.
- Boys do not have a bedroom culture like girls and so do not improve their communication skills to fit the demands of education.
- The curriculum, until recently, favoured girls, coursework in particular.
- The feminisation of education includes primary schools being staffed by a majority of female teachers who cannot control the behaviour of male pupils.
- Working class boys lack male role models.

QUICK TEST

1. Which sociologist argued that the results of boys and girls have more similarities than differences?

2. Ringrose argued that there has been an overreaction to the underachievement of working class boys in education. What term does she use to describe this overreaction?

3. Boys' rejection of school tasks such as reading are explained by these tasks being 'effeminate'. What does this term mean?

4. Mitsos and Browne argued that boys/men have suffered an identity crisis. What has caused this crisis in identity?

5. A 'bedroom culture' that trapped girls in their rooms had advantages for girls' success at school. Give the key advantage that girls gained from a 'bedroom culture'.

6. What explanation is given as to why boys regard reading as a female activity?

7. Which skills or qualities that boys have are, according to Tony Sewell, being ignored in education?

8. Why is the lack of male teachers in primary schools cause for concern in relation to boys' underachievement?

9. Which two sociologists disagreed that schools have become feminised?

10. What is meant by 'disciplinarian discourse'?

PRACTICE QUESTIONS

Item A

Schooling has shifted too far from a boy-bias to a girl-bias. This has left working class boys to struggle in a system that reprimands them for being dynamic and competitive. Some sociologists reject the idea that schools are biased in favour of girls and point to the narrowing of the gap overall between boys' and girls' academic achievements.

Question 1 (AS Level style): Applying material from Item A and your knowledge, evaluate the view that underachievement among working class boys is the result of the feminisation of education. (20 marks) **Spend 30 minutes on your response.**

HINTS TO HELP YOU RESPOND

In this response you are asked to 'evaluate'. This means looking at the advantages and disadvantages of the argument. You will note that the core debate within your essay here is about whether education favours girls' abilities more than boys'; of course the debate is narrowed to the underachievement of working class boys. You will need to assess all the factors that may affect both social class and gender achievement to support or undermine the core point of the question, that is, the feminisation of schools. Start with exploring what feminisation means: lack of male role models in education, a curriculum that favours girls' skills, and boys' rejection of schools through subculture (laddish culture). Once you have evaluated these points introduce other causes of underachievement of working class boys: personal identity, sexuality. Give evidence and examples of these points, evaluate these and link them directly to the core of the question. Your essay will show that there are a range of factors that are responsible for boys' underachievement; in fact, some regard the whole issue as a moral panic. Your conclusion can state that attainment in education is a complex issue that cuts across issues of ethnicity, gender and social class to involve personal identity and issues of sexuality. So to focus solely on class or gender ignores these other important issues.

Item B

A range of factors, both external and internal, can be examined to find the reasons behind the failure of working class boys in comparison to their counterparts. A subculture within schools of laddish behaviour has been blamed and this culture does extend beyond the school gates. The problems of securing employment after school and the low levels of literacy have also been key explanations.

Question 2 (A Level style): Applying material from Item B, analyse two explanations for working class boys' underachievement. (10 marks) **Spend 15 minutes on your response.**

HINTS TO HELP YOU RESPOND

You must use two points from the item so think carefully about where you will get your two points from here. You will note that the item mentions 'laddish behaviour'; this can be linked to the rejection of the ideal pupil image. The item also identifies 'securing employment'; this should be linked to the impact of globalisation and the 'identity crisis' that men feel. In analysing, discuss each point and explain it in depth, then question it. For example, you may discuss the crisis of masculine identity and the rejection of school values. Then question the focus on failing working class boys as a moral panic.

Ethnic Differences in Achievement: External Factors

Achievement Patterns

It is clear that some ethnic groups outperform others in the education system. Chinese pupils and those from Indian backgrounds achieve the highest grades at GCSE. In 2015 mixed-race and African Caribbean males achieved fewer A*–C grades at GCSE than any other group. Pakistani and Bangladeshi students underachieve in comparison to white students, but despite this they are more likely to go to university. African Caribbean students are 3·4 times more likely to face exclusion from school than white students.

There are a number of reasons that sociologists put forward in order to explain these patterns of achievement; many explanations involve factors from outside the education system **(external factors)** which we will focus upon in this topic.

Cultural Deprivation Theory

According to many sociologists some ethnic groups are not socialised effectively at home in order to do well in the education system. Differences in attitudes and values towards education across different cultures lead to differences in achievement in the education system causing minorities to be deprived of the culture needed for educational success.

Many sociologists suggest that black children are often socialised to take a **fatalistic attitude**, believing that they have little or no impact on their own success so there is little point in trying to achieve. These sociologists also cite the impact of **immediate gratification** as a cause for underachievement, with black students favouring rewards straight away rather than being willing to work hard through the education system for the reward of good grades at the end. With many black children coming from working class backgrounds we can attribute the external factors impacting on working class underachievement to explain the need for immediate gratification (see pages 12–13).

EVALUATION POINT

There is evidence to suggest that some ethnic minority groups are positively influenced by the culture of their families. Archer and Francis (2006) stated that parents of Chinese students often instil a desire to achieve in their children which helps them perform well in the education system.

New Right sociologist Charles Murray (1984) focused on the **family structure** among black communities; he saw the high levels of lone-parent families and the lack of a **male role model** as a cause of underachievement. This means that there is no successful male who is able to gainfully work to provide for the family for the child to model themselves on. Moynihan (1965) also suggested the family structure as a cause of underachievement for black students, though he maintained that the main impact is due to a culture of poverty that is reproduced in families without a male role model.

Pryce (1979) stated that the underachievement of black Caribbean students is due to the lasting **impact of slavery** and the low levels of self-esteem that occur as a result of this.

Some sociologists note the **language barrier** that students from immigrant families face when they come to the UK as a cause of underachievement with students failing to understand teachers and textbooks.

EVALUATION POINT

Driver and Ballard (1981) studied a number of students who spoke English as an additional language; they found that by the age of 16 the students had a similar standard of English to their peers who had been born and raised in the UK.

The language of black American students from poorer families has been blamed as a significant barrier to learning by Bereiter and Engelmann (1966). They stated that the language used by poorer black American students often lacks the correct use of grammar and structure.

Social Class and Ethnicity

Ruth Lupton (2004) highlighted the need to look further towards social class differences alongside ethnicity. After studying schools in working class areas with differing levels of ethnic diversity, she found that the behaviour in schools that were predominantly made up of white working class students was far poorer than that found within other ethnic groups. Lupton stated that the negative view of the education system that is held by many white working class parents has a significant impact on the educational performance of their children. Lupton found that ethnic minority parents were more likely to see the education system positively as they see its value as a means to advance in society.

Compensatory Educational Policies

Many **compensatory educational policies** have aimed to overcome factors that cause underperformance in the education system. These policies are often based on assumptions that one key factor is the cause of underachievement and fail to tackle the array of factors that may cause the underachievement. Many of these policies aim to tackle cultural deprivation. **Sure Start** is a compensatory educational policy that was introduced in the UK by the New Labour government in 1998. Sure Start centres aimed to tackle deprivation in many poorer areas by offering parenting classes among other measures. Despite the aims of Sure Start many local programmes failed to create links with some minority groups, for example failing to support children of travellers or of Bangladeshi origin.

Material Deprivation

It is clear that external factors other than cultural deprivation have an impact on the achievement of minority groups. Statistics show that many ethnic minority groups are likely to live in the poorest areas of the UK and in turn face **material deprivation** (a lack of the physical necessities that allow an individual to operate in today's society). Pakistanis, Bangladeshis and African Caribbeans are more likely to be economically disadvantaged than white students.

Research by Shelter (2004) found that in the social housing sector of London, up to one in five black minority ethnic households lived in overcrowded and cramped conditions in buildings that lacked sufficient rooms, which can impact on the space needed to complete homework effectively. Many sociologists would suggest that this is a direct result of racism in wider society. This **racism in society** also impacts on employment of ethnic minority groups, further creating a pattern of underachievement in poorer families.

SUMMARY

- There are a range of patterns which display different levels of achievement among ethnic minority groups in the education system.

- External factors (factors that occur outside the education system itself) are often blamed by sociologists for differences in achievement among ethnic minority groups.

- Cultural deprivation is often to blame as family structure, language barriers and the impact of slavery cause significant barriers to learning for some ethnic minority groups.

- Compensatory educational policies have aimed at reducing cultural deprivation among groups in the poorest areas of society. Sure Start is an example of a policy introduced by the Labour government.

- Many sociologists believe that we cannot separate the impact of social class on achievement from the issue of ethnic minority underachievement.

- Pakistanis, Bangladeshis and African Caribbeans are likely to experience material deprivation, impacting on their ability to achieve in the education system.

- Racism in wider society also holds significant value in causing ethnic minority underachievement with employment and housing affected among other factors.

QUICK TEST

1. Which compensatory educational policy was established by the New Labour government in 1998 to have a positive impact on cultural deprivation?

2. Which New Right sociologist suggested that a lack of a male role model in many black families has caused underachievement?

3. What is meant by a fatalistic attitude?

4. Which key term describes black students wanting rewards straight away rather than working through school for rewards of good grades at the end?

5. What did Pryce state as having a lasting impact on the achievement of black Caribbean students?

6. According to official statistics, which ethnic minority groups achieve the highest grades at GCSE?

7. Which key term describes the lack of physical necessities that Pakistani, Bangladeshi and African Caribbean students are likely to experience due to potentially being more economically disadvantaged than white students?

8. Which social pattern did Ruth Lupton believe we should look at alongside ethnicity?

9. What were the findings of Driver and Ballard (1981), when they studied students whose first language was not English?

10. According to Archer and Francis (2006), why do Chinese students achieve higher than most other ethnic groups?

PRACTICE QUESTIONS

Item A
Statistics show that there is a definite pattern within the educational performance of many ethnic minority groups in the UK education system. Many sociologists suggest that this is directly the result of family structure; others suggest that attitudes of ethnic minority students are to blame.

Question 1 (A Level style): Applying material from Item A, analyse two external factors that create ethnic differences in educational achievement. (10 marks) **Spend 15 minutes on your response.**

HINTS TO HELP YOU RESPOND
Here you must discuss two factors that are mentioned in the item. Be careful to pick them out before you start your response. You will see family structure as one (you could mention Charles Murray and the absence of a male role model). You will also find that you need to discuss attitudes of ethnic minority groups (here you could discuss fatalistic attitudes and the need for immediate gratification). Do not include an introduction; spend 7 minutes on each factor. You need to make sure that you fully explain how each one leads to underachievement. For example: 'Charles Murray (1984) stated that family structure among many black communities includes a high proportion of lone-parent families which lack a male role model. This has been blamed for the educational underachievement of black students as they do not have an example of a male role model within their family who has achieved well or promoted the importance of success in education. As a result of this many black students from lone-parent families underachieve.' Try to include detail in your paragraphs and follow the PEEL structure: point, evidence, explain and link back to the question.

Question 2 (AS Level style): Outline three ways in which cultural deprivation may cause differences in ethnic minority achievement in the education system. (6 marks) **Spend 9 minutes on your response.**

HINTS TO HELP YOU RESPOND
Your response here will be quite short. For each 'way' start a new line to show the examiner that you are outlining another point. You could discuss a range of cultural deprivation factors here: fatalistic attitudes, immediate gratification, family structure, language barriers, the impact of slavery, etc. Outlining your responses can be just two sentences each. For example: 'Many ethnic minority students are culturally deprived as they develop a need for immediate gratification. With many groups being affected by material deprivation, they adopt a hand-to-mouth existence wanting rewards straight away rather than working through the education system to be rewarded with good grades at the end of their studies.'

Ethnic Differences in Achievement: Internal Factors

You have already studied factors from outside the education system that sociologists believe cause the different patterns in achievement among ethnic groups. However, many sociologists believe that **internal factors** (factors within the education system) cause these patterns.

The internal factors that impact on achievement focus on how ethnic minority students are treated within the education system and the barriers that they face as a direct result of failures in the system itself. Gillborn and Youdell (2000) looked at one local education authority. They found that when entering primary school African Caribbean students were the highest achieving group, but by the time that they completed their GCSEs this group was the lowest achieving group of all ethnicities. This research suggests that factors in school must be to blame for the underachievement of ethnic minority groups.

Teacher Labelling

Labelling theory is the work of interactionist sociologists who examine the impact of small-scale interactions between individuals in society. Labelling theorists suggest that the labels given to minority ethnic students by teachers can have a dramatic impact on their success or failure in the education system. Gillborn (1990) stated that teachers are quick to negatively label black students and, as a result of this, African Caribbean students are more likely to be excluded from school, impacting on their achievement. Gillborn and Youdell (2000) found that teachers had **'racialised expectations'** of black students expecting them to threaten and challenge authority, thus leading to these students being treated negatively by teachers. As a result of these racist stereotypes, black students were more likely to be placed in lower sets or streams than their white peers. Louise Archer (2008) found that teachers saw the 'ideal pupil identity' as a white, asexual, middle class identity. She noted that black or white, overly sexualised, working class pupils had a 'demonised pupil identity' and were viewed as culturally deprived.

Cecile Wright (1992) looked at the negative impact of labelling on Asian students, contrasting that in the evaluation point. Wright found that in primary schools Asian students were treated differently to other groups. Teachers assumed that they would have low levels of English and as a result used basic restricted language in dialogue with them. Wright also found that teachers mispronounced Asian students' names and often ignored them in the classroom. As a result Asian students were prevented from taking part in class, which impacted on their self-esteem and faith in their own ability to succeed.

Subcultures as a Response to Racist Labelling

Teacher labelling and racism can impact on students in a variety of ways. Many students may form **subcultures** as a response to their labels. Tony Sewell (1998) looked into the range of responses shown by black boys to their racist labelling. At times this led the boys to form an **anti-school subculture** rejecting the values of the school itself. Sewell categorised the subcultural responses into four groups:

- The **rebels**. These students had a big impact and high profile in schools. They rejected the school rules and worked against the goal of educational success. These students focused mainly on getting their status through being a macho male in the street culture around them.

- The **retreatists**. This was a minority of students who tried to detach themselves from the school and also from the 'black subculture'. They became marginalised and isolated.
- The **innovators**. These students saw the value in learning; they wanted to succeed though were anti-school. These students worked to do well (innovating their own path to success), though rejected school itself.
- The **conformists** had the view that they wanted to succeed. These students aimed to socialise with students from a range of ethnicities to avoid their labels. They followed the school rules and values to aim for success.

Sewell noted that many teachers treated all black boys like the rebels, despite this only being a small proportion of students.

EVALUATION POINT

Not all ethnic minority students who are labelled passively accept their label. The view that all labels impact on students to whom they are applied is simply too **deterministic**. Mary Fuller (1984) researched a group of black Year 11 girls who were achieving highly at a London comprehensive school. The girls found success by working hard without appearing to do so; through this they were able to socialise with others in the anti-school subculture and succeed at the same time. In contrast to this Heidi Mirza (1992) noted that at times black girls refused to engage with members of staff who they knew had negatively labelled them; this meant that they failed to secure guidance and help, restricting their chance of success.

Institutional Racism

Sociologists suggest that the level of underachievement identified in ethnic minority groups cannot simply be due to the individual racism of teachers themselves. These sociologists note that

the education system is based around a system of institutional racism. Critical Race Theorists see this **institutional racism** to be deeply ingrained in the practices and policies of the education system as a whole. They cite a number of ways in which the system is institutionally racist.

Troyna and Williams (1986) stated that the education system delivers an **ethnocentric curriculum**, giving priority to the English language and white culture. This is an example of institutional racism which causes ethnic minority students to see themselves as disconnected from the curriculum that they are taught. Leon Tikly (2006) supported this view of an ethnocentric curriculum. He surveyed black children in 30 comprehensive schools and found that they felt isolated as a result of a lack of black role models in the curriculum.

Gillborn (1997) noted that **marketisation** policies (which require parents to select schools for their children) have served to act as a form of institutional racism. These policies have given schools a chance to be more selective about which students they accept, allowing schools to favour certain ethnicities over others.

Tikly (2006) argued that black students are less likely to be identified as gifted and talented by schools, which means that talented black students may fail to be stretched effectively by teachers, causing them to underachieve.

EVALUATION POINT

It is clear that no one single factor can be blamed for the ethnic minority underachievement as a whole. Here you can contrast the internal factors that cause underachievement with the external factors of cultural deprivation and material deprivation outlined on pages 12–13.

SUMMARY

- Ethnic minority underachievement may be the result of internal factors (processes within the education system).

- Many teachers negatively label black students causing negative responses from the students themselves and a sense of isolation.

- Tony Sewell looked at the subcultural responses of ethnic minority students who had been negatively labelled and categorised the responses into four types: rebels, retreatists, innovators and conformists.

- Institutional racism in the education system has been blamed on the underachievement of ethnic minority groups. Critical Race Theorists see this as deeply ingrained in the system as a whole.

- There is an ethnocentric curriculum in the UK, which focuses mainly on white culture. This institutional racism isolates minorities and disconnects them from the content that they are taught.

- Marketisation policies cause difficulties for some ethnic minority students when selecting an effective school. Schools are able to be more selective over which students they accept; this institutional racism causes many ethnic minority students to end up in failing schools.

QUICK TEST

1. Which term is used to describe the subject content taught across schools which focuses mainly on white culture?

2. What do interactionist sociologists focus on which they suggest causes the underachievement of ethnic minority students, particularly black students?

3. Which sociologist looked at four response categories that occur as a result of teachers' racist labelling?

4. Which response to negative labelling involved students creating their own ways to succeed without the help of teachers?

5. According to Gillborn, which policies have further served to act as a form of institutional racism in order for schools to be more selective about the minority students that they accept?

6. What key word could be used to describe the view that all students passively accept their labels?

7. According to Cecile Wright, what assumptions did teachers make about Asian pupils?

8. What did Leon Tikly's study highlight the lack of in the curriculum?

9. Which sociologist studied successful black girls who had created their own chances for success without fully engaging with teachers?

10. According to Gillborn (1990) what is more likely to happen to African Caribbean students than other groups?

PRACTICE QUESTIONS

Item A
Patterns in achievement across ethnic minority groups highlight the fact that many ethnic minority groups are at a significant disadvantage in the education system. Some students may fall victim to teacher racism and the negative labels placed on them. Other students may be affected by the institutional racism that many sociologists believe to be at the root of the education system. Some students may respond by attempting to succeed despite the racism in the education system.

Question 1 (A Level style): Applying material from Item A and your knowledge, evaluate the view that ethnic minority underachievement is the result of processes within schools. (30 marks) **Spend 45 minutes on your response.**

HINTS TO HELP YOU RESPOND
Here you need to examine the internal factors that cause ethnic minority underachievement. Be precise in your explanation, ensuring that you use sociologists to support your key arguments of teacher racism, labelling and institutional racism. Your response must show a clear thought pattern; create a 5 minute plan before starting your response, and consider which evaluative points fit where. In evaluating internal factors, you will need to use external factors. For example, when you explain teacher racism, you can use racism in society (see the Shelter research on pages 32–33) to explain that teachers may simply be a product of the racist society around them. Develop the points from the item and let the examiner know you are doing this by using terms such as: 'in Item A…' or 'the item suggests…' It will be difficult to be conclusive in stating that ethnic minority underachievement is simply a result of internal factors. You can conclude that all factors must be taken into account.

Question 2 (AS Level style): Define the term 'ethnocentric curriculum'. (2 marks) **Spend no more than 3 minutes on your response.**

HINTS TO HELP YOU RESPOND
With a 2 mark question, your response must be short and precise. By defining a term, state what the term is without using any words from the term itself, e.g. 'The ethnocentric curriculum is the term given to the subject content delivered across all schools which prioritises white culture.'

Question 3 (AS Level style): Using one example, briefly explain how institutional racism occurs in the education system. (2 marks) **Spend no more than 3 minutes on your response.**

HINTS TO HELP YOU RESPOND
Again here, you will need to be short and precise with your response. Start by stating one example of institutional racism and then expand briefly to explain how this is a racist act within the system, e.g. 'Marketisation policies put in place by the New Right government in 1988 mean that schools can be selective over which students they accept. Schools have the ability to exclude ethnic minority students, forcing them to attend poorer performing schools with lower chance of success. This is institutionally racist as it places ethnic minority students at a disadvantage.'

Educational Policy 1944–2010

'**Educational policies**' are rules and guidelines put in place by the government when controlling the education system. Many educational policies aim to remove any inequality that may occur within the system, from gender inequality to social class inequality. Most policies aim to provide equal opportunities and choice for students. Some educational policies have been more successful than others.

1944 The Tripartite System

In 1944 educational policies were introduced that aimed to make the education system a '**meritocracy**'; this means that everyone has an equal chance of success based on their ability and effort. The **1944 Education Act** introduced the **tripartite system**, aimed at giving all students an opportunity to show their true abilities. This system involved each student taking an **11+** exam at the end of their primary schooling.

Students who passed the 11+ exam went to **grammar schools**. Here they would be taught an academic curriculum and given the chance to work towards higher education (university). The students who attended grammar schools tended to be middle class. Middle class students could afford access to private tutors, allowing them to be more prepared for the 11+ exam.

If a student failed the 11+ exam, they would go to a **secondary modern school**. In these schools the curriculum was based around manual labour. Secondary modern schools were mainly attended by working class students.

There was also a third type of school called a 'technical school', though these only existed in a few areas. The system was really only based around grammar and secondary modern schools.

EVALUATION POINT

Rather than creating a meritocracy, the tripartite system created a class divide between the middle and working class. Middle class students were offered more opportunities than working class students, pushing them further apart. To pass the 11+ girls had to achieve a higher number of marks than boys, which also caused a gender gap in achievement. The system ignored the fact that a child's background has a dramatic impact on their ability to perform in the 11+ exam.

1965 Comprehensive Schools

In the majority of areas **comprehensive** schools were introduced in 1965. The aim of the comprehensive system was to have one type of school which all pupils would attend. This would create a more meritocratic system as all students would receive the same schooling regardless of social class and gender. The 11+ no longer existed in the majority of areas, and secondary modern schools and grammar schools were replaced by comprehensives.

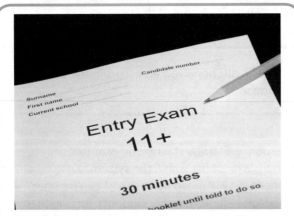

When the 1944 Education Act introduced the tripartite system, students who passed the 11+ exam could go to grammar schools.

The decision as to whether or not to abolish grammar schools was down to local education authorities. In some conservative areas grammar schools were kept. This meant that the comprehensive system was not truly meritocratic as students at grammar schools still received selective schooling in an environment where all other students in attendance had passed the entrance exam. Functionalists would suggest that comprehensive schools were inclusive and created meritocracy. Marxists would disagree, stating that comprehensive schools simply reproduced and legitimised class inequality through the external and internal factors placing working class students at a disadvantage (see pages 12–13 and 16–17).

1988 Marketisation

The Conservative government made radical changes to the education system by introducing the **Education Reform Act 1988**. The aim of this act was to raise standards within schools by creating an education market in which schools would compete against each other in order for parents to select them for their child to attend. This change, to add competition between schools, is known as **'marketisation'**. The Conservative government also wanted to reduce the role of the state in controlling education.

In order for schools to compete against each other new measures were put in place, by which parents could compare schools. These included **Ofsted** inspections in which schools were awarded a grade based on performance in a number of categories, including the effectiveness of teaching and learning. The government also introduced **league tables** as a means of comparing schools by the exam results of the students who attended. The aim of this was to create a **'parentocracy'** where parents would be able to choose the right school for their child. Schools were allocated funds based on how many students they could attract, which is called **'formula funding'**.

As a result of this, it was in schools' interests to attract as many students as they could, driving up standards to be more competitive.

Not all parents are equally equipped when selecting a school for their child. Gewirtz suggested that middle class parents have an advantage in selecting schools as they have the cultural capital that the school system prefers and therefore a better knowledge of the selection procedures. Gewirtz called the middle class **'privileged skilled choosers'** of schools. Working class parents will often select the most convenient, or closest, school. Gewirtz labelled them as **'disconnected-local choosers'**. This means that working class students are likely to end up in less effective schools, further creating a class gap in achievement. League tables also encourage schools to create an 'A*–C economy', focusing on improving the performance of students who are likely to boost their headline figures. Many working class students are placed in lower sets and are often neglected as they have less chance of improving the school's league table position.

1997–2010 New Labour Policies

The New Labour government continued to support marketisation and competition among schools. In order to create meritocracy, they introduced **compensatory educational policies** which aimed at reducing inequality.

These policies included an **Aim Higher** programme which worked towards raising the aspirations of working class students to attend higher education (university). They also introduced **Education Action Zones**. In deprived areas, schools were given resources and funding to provide students with equipment and opportunities that they may not have had due to **material deprivation**.

Students who stayed on after the age of 16 were entitled to **Education Maintenance Allowance (EMA)** payments if their home income was below a certain level. This was aimed at reducing the need for **immediate gratification** and keeping working class students in education. **City academies** were built in deprived areas in order to provide a new start for struggling schools.

EVALUATION POINT

Alongside the introduction of EMA payments to encourage students to stay in education the New Labour government introduced higher university **tuition fees**, which discouraged working class students from attending higher education. The New Labour government still allowed private education in fee paying schools to exist; many privileged middle class students would attend these and have an advantage over the working class. EMA was abolished in 2010 meaning that its impact on equality was only brief.

QUICK TEST

1. What is the name given to the education system introduced in 1944?

2. What is meant by the term 'marketisation'?

3. In 1944, which exam did all students take in order to decide which school they would attend?

4. Name two features used by parents to compare schools in a marketised system.

5. What does EMA stand for?

6. What did Gewirtz label working class parents as when selecting a school for their child?

7. What is meant by the term 'formula funding'?

8. Which key term describes a system that is fair in which all have an equal chance of success based on ability and effort?

9. What did the Aim Higher programme, introduced by the New Labour government, focus on achieving?

10. Which schools did students attend if they did not pass the 11+ test in 1944?

SUMMARY

- 'Educational policies' are rules and guidelines put in place by the government when controlling the education system.

- In 1944 the tripartite system ensured that every child took the 11+ exam. Students who passed attended grammar schools (these were mainly middle class students). If a student failed they would attend a secondary modern school (these were mainly working class students).

- Comprehensive schools were introduced in 1965 to create one type of school for all to attend. In some conservative areas grammar schools were retained.

- The Education Reform Act 1988 marketised schools to create a parentocracy in order to drive up standards in schools. Middle class parents were better at selecting the best schools for their children.

- The New Labour government in 1997 created compensatory educational policies to further reduce inequality in the education system. These were often flawed due to other barriers to progress that still existed.

PRACTICE QUESTIONS

Question 1 (A Level style): Outline two criticisms of the marketised education system. (4 marks) **Spend 6 minutes on your response.**

HINTS TO HELP YOU RESPOND
Select two criticisms to outline, e.g. working class parents are not effective school choosers, grammar schools still existed in some areas. Start each criticism on a new line and simply explain it briefly, ideally using no more than two sentences. For example: 'Marketisation caused a wider class divide as working class parents are often disconnected-local choosers of schools. This means that working class students are more likely to attend the closest school, rather than the best school for their needs.'

Question 2 (AS Level style): Define the term 'parentocracy'. (2 marks) **Spend no more than 3 minutes on your response.**

HINTS TO HELP YOU RESPOND
One sentence is enough for a 2 mark question. Simply note what a parentocracy is.

Question 3 (AS Level style): Outline and explain two ways in which educational policies have served to create inequality. (10 marks) **Spend 15 minutes on your response.**

HINTS TO HELP YOU RESPOND
First find two effects that you could discuss. You could discuss marketisation and how it caused privileged skilled choosers from middle class backgrounds to be at an advantage. You could also discuss the introduction of tuition fees for university entrance. Place your points into a PEEL paragraph (point, evidence, explain and link to the question). For example: 'The introduction of marketisation saw the introduction of measures which allowed schools to compete against each other for parents to select them for their children to attend. Ofsted and league tables were just two measures that allowed parents to judge schools. Parents with middle class backgrounds were better equipped to judge and select schools as they were more aware of the selection process. They were able to act as privileged skilled choosers. This served to create class inequality between working and middle class students in the education system.'

Educational Policy 2010–2016

Following the New Labour government, which introduced compensatory educational policies and served from 1997 to 2010, the **Coalition government** was formed as no political party obtained a majority vote. This government consisted of Conservative and Liberal Democrat politicians.

As Prime Minister of the Coalition government David Cameron aimed to increase **competition** between schools and add **'innovation'** into the education system. He stated that the education system should be further removed from the state, with government involvement being reduced in order to raise standards. The comprehensive system of one school for all was to be dismantled, with a focus now upon **marketisation** and the privatisation of the education system.

The Coalition government promoted **academisation** to all schools, aiming for every school to become an academy. Schools that became academies would have more control over their own budgets and also over the curriculum that was taught. Within a year, over 11% of all secondary schools in England had become academies. By 2013, this number was 48%.

EVALUATION POINT

By encouraging schools to become academies the Coalition government served to **reduce central control** over schools. This meant that schools became less accountable to the government and caused a further disparity in standards between schools. In turn, a change in standards across schools could impact on the class gap in achievement with working class students more likely to end up in failing schools as a result of their parents being 'disconnected-local choosers'.

Free schools were promoted at this time. These schools could be run by parents, teachers, businesses or even faith groups. The aim of free schools was to further provide parents with power over the education system. If parents and teachers had little confidence in local state-run schools, and their ability to provide for the children in their area, they were able to establish their own schools.

EVALUATION POINT

Higham (2014) suggested that the majority of proposals to start free schools focused on areas other than providing social equality, favouring middle class aspirations rather than those of working class families. As a result Higham noted that he believed free schools to potentially have a **'stratification effect'**, reinforcing the class gap in achievement. Other research suggested that free schools are reluctant to take working class pupils.

Stephen Ball suggested that Coalition education policies have caused a **'fragmented centralisation'**. As there are now new types of school and more variety, Ball argued that the education system has become fragmented, specifically in comparison to the comprehensive system. Ball also questioned the centralised power that the government has in which it can make such sweeping and radical changes to the education system.

Since the forming of the Coalition government in 2010 vast spending cuts have impacted on the success of a number of educational policies already in place. Many New Labour policies like Sure Start and the Educational Maintenance Allowance have been reduced or removed. There has also been a significant increase in university **tuition fees**. This increase in tuition fees has further caused reluctance for working class students to enter higher education, counteracting programmes like Aim Higher.

EVALUATION POINT

Spending cuts in the education system have served to create a less meritocratic education system. Many compensatory education policies have been removed or heavily impacted on in order to save costs. This will create a further gap in achievement between working class and middle class students.

Privatising Education

Both the Coalition government (2010–2015) and the Conservative government (2015–) have encouraged the **privatisation** of the education system. The education system has become an increasingly appealing way for businesses to make money. Private companies have become more involved in the education system, from running some courses to providing careers advice. The education system provides a lucrative environment in which companies can make significant profits due to state funding. Many large companies have now taken control over local schools, or chains of schools. For example, the VT Group, which started out building ships for the Royal Navy, now operates a number of schools in London. This privatisation of schools further fuels marketisation and competition with companies aiming to attract more customers (parents).

Many businesses have been given a platform to promote their products across schools, with schools in England having brands such as Starbucks selling their products alongside the school caterers. Schools also affiliate with brands through the collecting of vouchers in exchange for products such as sports equipment. There are often very few advantages of schools being involved in these partnerships, and they often gain very little financial benefit. This impact of the private sector on schools is known as the **'cola-isation'** of schools.

EVALUATION POINT

Marxists would suggest that the privatisation of schools simply allows opportunities for the bourgeoisie (or ruling class) to exploit the working class and increase their profits. There is now a real level of confusion over who exactly is running state-funded schools. Some are controlled by parents and teachers, others operated by private businesses and some by the state itself. This fragmentation has caused further possible inconsistencies in the standard of education provided for students.

SUMMARY

- In 2010 the Coalition government aimed to add more competition and innovation into the education system.

- Schools were encouraged to become academies; this meant that they would have more control over their budgets and curriculum.

- Academisation served to reduce central control over schools, leading to differences in standards across schools and further fuelling a class gap in achievement.

- The Coalition government introduced free schools that could be established by groups such as parents, teachers and businesses.

- Ball argued that a 'fragmented centralisation' of the education system has occurred with many different types of schools and an increased impact from central government.

- Many existing compensatory educational policies were impacted on by budget cuts. These cuts saw the introduction of higher university tuition fees.

- The Coalition and Conservative governments from 2010–present have promoted privatisation of the education system with many businesses and companies taking ownership and control of educational facilities.

- With an increase in partnerships with private companies the 'cola-isation' of schools has occurred. More companies are establishing and promoting brands within the education system.

QUICK TEST

1. Which two political parties formed the Coalition government in 2010?

2. What is meant by the 'privatisation' of the education system?

3. How did Ball describe a system which now has many different types of school, yet experiences significant impact from government policies?

4. Name a compensatory educational policy that has been affected by the Coalition government's raise in university tuition fees.

5. Which term describes a rise in the link between schools and brands?

6. Which type of school did the Coalition government encourage, removing local authority control over school budgets?

7. What effect did Higham suggest free schools will have owing to the majority of free school applications neglecting the aim of social equality?

8. Which type of sociologist would question the privatisation of the education system, as it simply promotes opportunities for the ruling class to make large profits?

9. Why might parents or teachers set up a free school?

10. Which private company started out building ships for the Royal Navy and now operates a number of schools in London?

PRACTICE QUESTIONS

Question 1 (AS Level style): Define the term 'Cola-isation of schools'. (2 marks) **Spend no more than 3 minutes on your response.**

> **HINTS TO HELP YOU RESPOND**
> Be short with your response. Two sentences will do here. Describe the increased involvement of brands in education; you may even use an example (e.g. Starbucks) to explain your definition.

Question 2 (AS Level style): Using one example, briefly explain how 'academisation' may cause a further class gap in achievement. (2 marks) **Spend no more than 3 minutes on your response.**

> **HINTS TO HELP YOU RESPOND**
> Select a way in which academies create inequality. Your response needs to be short. For example: 'With reduced central control over academies, standards of education provided across schools can be different. As a result of working class parents acting as 'disconnected-local choosers' their children are likely to attend the least successful schools.'

> **Item A**
> In 2010 the Coalition government set to establish educational policies aimed at raising competition and innovation in the education system. The introduction of academies and free schools meant that the role of the state in controlling schools was reduced. Academies were able to control their own budgets and curriculum. Many sociologists suggest that the encouragement of schools to become academies has created inequality in the standards of education provided across the education system as a whole, which in turn has served to increase a class gap in educational achievement.

Question 3 (A Level style): Applying material from Item A and your knowledge, evaluate the claim that Coalition policies have served to increase social inequality. (30 marks) **Spend 45 minutes on your response.**

> **HINTS TO HELP YOU RESPOND**
> Start by explaining what Coalition educational policies were. For example, academies, free schools, privatisation. Also mention increased marketisation. Question each of these in terms of its success. Use arguments to suggest that the policies created differences in standards and therefore a class gap in achievement. Use Higham in your evaluation of free schools. Use Marxists in your evaluation of privatisation. Draw upon the Coalition government increasing marketisation, mention how formula funding means that working class students are likely to end up in schools that have less money. Discuss how Coalition policies have impacted on the compensatory educational policies such as Aim Higher. As you mention the policies, evaluate them one by one so that your evaluative points are spread throughout your essay rather than saved for the end.

Key Research Methods in General

Theoretical Factors Affecting a Sociologist's Choice of Research Method

Sociologists have a wide range of research methods available to them. A variety of factors affect the sociologist's choice of which method to use. One main factor is the sociologist's **theoretical perspective**. When looking into methodology there are two theoretical perspectives that must be considered, positivism and interpretivism.

Positivists favour **quantitative data** (numerical). This data allows positivists to find patterns of correlation to discover **cause and effect** relationships. These correlations allow positivists to find **social facts**, much like the laws of cause and effect that you would find through scientific research. They aim to reveal the underlying causes of human behaviour. Quantitative methods allow the sociologist to remain **objective**, which means that their own views will not impact on the research.

Research methods such as official statistics, questionnaires and structured research (like experiments or structured interviews) are favoured by positivists as they gather quantitative data and are more likely to be **representative**. As a sociologist is rarely able to study the whole of the population which they aim to research, they use a **sample** of the population. Large samples are more likely to represent the population being studied. These methods are often less time consuming and in turn useful for studying larger groups of people.

Positivists like to measure patterns of behaviour over time. Because of this they prefer methods that are **reliable** (easy to replicate). Methods that follow a **standardised procedure** are the most reliable as they allow the researcher to follow the same procedure to test a hypothesis (statement being tested) again and again.

EVALUATION POINT

Interpretivists disagree with the main positivist goals of representativeness and reliability. They believe that quantitative data neglects to gather detail about the meanings individuals have for their own actions, failing to discover why people act in the ways they do. Interpretivists argue that there is no objective way to study society.

Interpretivists favour **qualitative data** (words, thoughts and meanings). Qualitative data allows interpretivists to conduct research which is **valid**, which means that it gathers the truth behind social situations. As a result of this, interpretivists favour unstructured methods, such as unstructured interviews and participant observation. These methods allow the sociologist to develop a deeper understanding of the individuals studied and therefore gather an insight into the meanings behind their actions. This helps them achieve 'verstehen', an empathetic understanding of human behaviour.

EVALUATION POINT

Positivists believe that small-scale research which aims for validity is not useful and suggest that the small samples used for qualitative research are not suitable to make generalisations from. Positivists argue that qualitative data fails to prove social facts as it does not reveal cause and effect relationships.

Practical Factors Affecting a Sociologist's Choice of Research Method

Time available to the sociologist can have a large influence over their choice of method. Many quantitative methods are swift to conduct and analyse, such as questionnaires. In contrast, the depth needed to gather validity in many qualitative methods is often time consuming.

Research methods that are time consuming require large amounts of money. Methods that require specialist equipment are also costly. The **finance** available to the sociologist will be reliant upon their **source of funding**. Large-scale research is also costly, but this can be resolved by using a smaller sample. Funding bodies may also prefer the sociologist to use specific methods, restricting the research at times.

Traits and skills of the sociologist can prove to be practical advantages or disadvantages. Sociologists may have to be trained to conduct certain types of research. Some sociologists may prove more vulnerable than others depending on the research area. A sociologist's gender, ethnicity and social class can all be important factors when gaining access to a group to study.

Research and Ethics

Due to the nature of sociology, researchers must take into account the impact of their research on the individuals involved and also on wider society. There are a number of **ethical considerations** that must take place. Sociologists should gather **informed consent** from their participants; those involved should know exactly what the research involves and also its aims.

Participants have the right to remain **anonymous** in any research. They should be secure in the knowledge that their details will not be published or used without permission.

EVALUATION POINT

By informing participants of the research, the process itself may become flawed. Participants may change their behaviour as they become aware of being studied (known as the 'Hawthorne effect'). This is particularly an issue in covert research where the sociologist's identity and aim are intentionally kept from the participants. **Covert** methods do, however, produce more valid data.

The sociologist should aim to avoid any **physical or psychological harm** to participants. They should also take extra care when researching **vulnerable groups** within genders, age groups and ethnicities.

Conducting Sociological Research

Sociologists must develop an aim or hypothesis (statement to be proven or disproven) to study. Once they have done this the sociologist must **'operationalise concepts'**, which simply means identifying exactly how they can measure their hypothesis. For example, a study that looks at the social class of students may use whether or not students receive free school meals as an indicator of social class. A sociologist may then trial their research by running a **pilot study**.

How Sociologists Gather a Sample

Sociologists select a sample of people to research from the wider population. The group from which they take their sample is called a **'sampling frame'** (an example could simply be the electoral register). Samples should aim to reflect the population being studied in order to be representative. Positivists are more concerned with having a large representative sample than interpretivists.

There are several types of sampling to consider. **Systematic sampling** will follow a structure, e.g. selecting every fifth person from the sampling frame. **Quota sampling** is when the researcher has a certain type of person to research and they simply select the first number of people who fit the criteria, e.g. the first 30 males aged 20–40. **Stratified sampling** requires the researcher to mirror the characteristics of the population in their sample ensuring that their sample is a mirrored smaller version of the sampling frame, e.g. if 45% of the sampling frame is male then 45% of the sample must be male. **Random sampling** is when the sociologist ensures that everyone in the sampling frame has an equal chance of being in the sample. For example, they may draw names from a hat.

SUMMARY

- Theoretical perspective can influence a sociologist's choice of research method. Positivists and interpretivists have different priorities.

- Positivists prefer quantitative data which allows their research to be representative and reliable in order to find cause and effect relationships.

- Interpretivists prefer qualitative data which allows them to conduct valid research aiming to find the meanings which individuals give for their own actions.

- Practical factors can impact on research. These include: time, finance funding source, cost and the sociologist's identity.

- Ethical considerations must be taken into account with research. These include: gathering informed consent, vulnerable groups, participants remaining anonymous, avoiding physical and psychological harm. Covert research conflicts with many of these.

- When conducting research sociologists need to operationalise concepts. Once this is completed they may run a pilot study to eradicate any issues.

- Sociologists may use: systematic sampling, quota sampling, stratified sampling or random sampling in order to select their sample from the sampling frame.

QUICK TEST

1. Which theoretical perspective prefers to use quantitative data?

2. What is the main goal of an interpretivist?

3. What is meant by the term 'reliability'?

4. Name two practical factors that may affect a sociologist in their research.

5. What should sociologists gather from their participants before conducting research on them?

6. Which type of sampling would follow a pattern and select, for example, every third person from the sampling frame?

7. What term is given to research where the sociologist's identity and purpose are unknown to the participants?

8. What is a 'pilot study'?

9. Which term is used for the process of placing a hypothesis into something that is measurable? For example, measuring social class by looking at family income.

10. What type of sampling would gather a certain number of individuals who match the researcher's criteria before stopping?

PRACTICE QUESTIONS

Question 1 (A Level style): Outline and explain two ways in which ethical considerations may affect sociologists' work. (10 marks) **Spend 15 minutes on your response.**

HINTS TO HELP YOU RESPOND

You need to divide your response equally between two ethical considerations. You can select from any in the topic (gathering informed consent, vulnerable groups, participants remaining anonymous, avoiding physical or psychological harm). Aim for two PEEL paragraphs (point, evidence, explain and link to the question). For example: 'Sociologists should ensure that their participants give informed consent before they take part in their research. Giving informed consent shows they are aware that they are being researched and are also aware of the research purpose. This is useful as it prevents the participant from being deceived. However, once a participant is aware that they are being researched they may change their behaviour. Informed consent is vital in ensuring that research is ethically sound. However, this may impact on the validity of the research.'

Question 2 (AS Level style): Outline two practical problems faced in sociological research. (2 marks) **Spend 3 minutes on your response.**

HINTS TO HELP YOU RESPOND

Two simple points are all that is needed here. State each practical problem on a separate line and add a quick sentence explaining it. For example: 'Many research methods are time consuming and sociologists may need to conduct their research swiftly. Qualitative methods require more depth and therefore often take more time.'

Question 3 (AS Level style): Outline two theoretical factors taken into account when conducting sociological research. (2 marks) **Spend 3 minutes on your response.**

HINTS TO HELP YOU RESPOND

In this response you must mention factors that are linked to theoretical perspectives. The two perspectives you need to use are positivist and interpretivist. Consider the factors impacting on the perspective for your response. Two simple points, started on separate lines are needed. Use reliability, representativeness or validity. For example: 'Positivists are more likely to use research methods that are representative. They may do this because they can gather more data making it easier to map a cause and effect relationship.'

Education as a Research Context

In the exam you will be asked to evaluate the usefulness of research methods in studying aspects of the education system. The education system is a diverse and complex area for sociologists to research. Within it there are a number of different roles and settings which sociologists may need to research, each with its own positives and negatives.

Roles within Schools

The two main roles which sociologists research in education are that of the **pupil** and the **teacher**. Pupils are often difficult to research as they are a **vulnerable group** due to their age and, as a result of this, ethical considerations must be taken into account and there must be **informed consent** from a parent or guardian.

When researching students, sociologists may encounter issues of validity. If a student is a member of an **anti-school subculture**, they may view the researcher as a teacher and therefore reject their research. Certain pupils may be more difficult than others to include in a sample; for example, students who **truant** school will not be as accessible as those who don't, as they cannot be studied reliably on the school site.

The **language** used when carrying out primary research (that is, conducted first hand by the sociologist themself) must suit the pupil so that they understand what is being asked of them and can respond clearly. This is often difficult to gauge as **pupils' understanding** varies widely across age and ability groups.

Because pupils are trained to obey teachers in schools, researchers may find that students respond in a manner that might reflect the views of their teacher (or be based around their view of how the teacher would like them to respond). This may impact on validity as students will fail to give their own honest opinions.

EVALUATION POINT

There are positives to studying pupils. As pupils attend schools, they can be conveniently studied in the same location at the one time. Because pupils are regularly being scrutinised by teachers they will be used to being researched and, therefore, may be more open to participating.

Teachers are regularly observed and their performance is scrutinised (for example by **Ofsted inspections**) and as a result they are often reluctant to participate in sociological research. They may also already feel under **pressure** from a high workload. Teachers are in control of their own classrooms and may not be willing to allow a sociologist access to observe classroom interactions.

EVALUATION POINT

As teachers are used to being studied the experience is not alien to them, and as a result they may be more willing to take part in sociological research.

Because teacher performance is measured in schools, teachers are used to **managing the impressions** that others have of them. **Overt** methods (where the researcher's identity and purpose are known) may cause the teacher to manipulate the research by changing their behaviour to impress. Therefore, observation of teachers may be better taking place 'backstage', outside class where teachers are less used to being observed. This will result in higher levels of validity.

Educational Research Settings

Research in classrooms is often difficult as these are highly **controlled environments**. Pupils and teachers work to a regular routine, which means that there is often less opportunity to measure exactly what pupils and teachers think and feel in class, as the nature of most lessons means that time to discuss and evaluate feelings is restricted. A mixture of methods which take place inside and outside the classroom would produce much more valid findings. The classroom is a small setting and class sizes rarely reach more than 32 pupils, which means that samples observed within the classroom are small and lack representativeness of the sampling frame as a whole. Because of setting and streaming class groups often vary in ability, which means that studying more than one group is often needed to gather findings for a range of ability groups. To gain access to the classroom sociologists must obtain permission from a range of **gatekeepers** including head teachers, teaching unions, teachers and laws that protect children.

There is a wide and growing range of **types of school** for sociologists to research. This means that research should be large scale to be representative of each of these establishments. School governors and head teachers act as gatekeepers and are often reluctant to place their staff and students under undue stress and time pressure by allowing sociological research to take place.

Schools produce their own **data for measurement of students' performance**. To outsiders such as parents of prospective students, schools will be highly selective over which data they publish as the marketised system forces schools to compete against each other for pupil places.

Many processes and social situations that occur within schools will often be off limits to the sociologist. Head teachers may not allow sociologists to observe meetings with parents, particularly when complaints against the school are being dealt with.

Researching Parents

Parents play a large part in the socialisation and education of their child, and as a result they are often keen to show their parenting abilities and actions in a positive light. This means that they may not be completely truthful about their actions, causing issues with validity. Some parental groups are more likely to be willing to take part in sociological research. Parents who are middle class and **pro-school** are more likely to respond than those who are working class and **anti-school**. Parental permission is required for many areas of research around the child, and parents will be reluctant to give permission when they feel that the research may impact negatively on their child.

Some parental groups are more likely to be willing to take part in sociological research.

SUMMARY

- There is a range of roles and settings in the education system for sociologists to research.
- To research pupils, informed consent from parents or guardians must be obtained as they are vulnerable due to their age.
- Pupils from anti-school subcultures may aim to show schools and education in a negative light.
- Care must be taken over the language used in research to ensure that students across ability and age groups understand.
- Teachers are used to being scrutinised by agencies such as Ofsted. As a result they may be reluctant to allow a sociologist to research them and may manage the impressions that others have of them.
- Classrooms are a controlled environment with limited numbers of students to research, impacting on the validity and representativeness of the research.
- Head teachers, governors, parents, teaching unions and teachers all act as gatekeepers when researching education.
- Schools are likely to present data that shows them in a positive light due to marketisation.
- Middle class pro-school parents are more likely to take part in research than working class anti-school parents.

QUICK TEST

1. What must sociologists gather from parents and guardians before conducting research on pupils?

2. Why might pupils be considered a vulnerable group to research?

3. Give an example of an agency that scrutinises teachers and their performance.

4. Why is it difficult to map trends in gauging pupils' understanding throughout research?

5. What causes difficulty when attempting to conduct a representative study of the education system?

6. Which parents are most likely to actively engage with sociological research?

7. Why might truancy cause issues for a sociologist researching pupils?

8. Which group of students are most likely to aim to show their teachers and schooling in a negative light?

9. Why are schools selective about the data that they show to sociologists?

10. What is meant by the term 'overt'?

PRACTICE QUESTION

Item A

Teachers often label students according to their opinion of how the child fits their view of the 'ideal pupil'. This labelling often leads pupils to identify with other pupils who are treated in a similar way. These groups of students may share values which reject those of the education system and become an anti-school subculture. These students are more likely to disrupt learning in class, truant school and also lack respect for authority figures in school.

Sociologists may use observation to research pupils within anti-school subcultures. By using observation sociologists are able to witness the behaviour of students from anti-school subcultures first hand.

Question 1 (AS and A Level style): Applying material from Item A and your knowledge of research methods, evaluate the strengths and limitations of observation for studying pupil members of anti-school subcultures. (20 marks) **Spend 30 minutes on your response.**

HINTS TO HELP YOU RESPOND

In this response you will need to use key material from pages 64–65. The item is extremely valuable here and gives you key hooks to mention in your response. Read through the item pulling out information about the nature of anti-school subcultures and the nature of observation.

To obtain a high standard of response you must make direct links between the nature of the research method specifically linked to the context of education, in this case observation specifically to study anti-school subcultures. It may not be possible to make every point a direct link, though the more detailed and direct your links are the better your response will be.

For example: 'As Item A suggests, observation allows a sociologist an opportunity to witness the behaviour of pupil members of anti-school subcultures first hand. This means that the sociologist is able to observe patterns of behaviour that show the pupils' disregard for the values of the education system for themselves and may also be the only way to obtain valid data as students may lie in interviews. Observation may not be useful in researching anti-school subcultures as pupils from anti-school subcultures are more likely to truant from school, as a result of which the sociologist may not find the pupil in a classroom setting to observe them. The sociologist may be forced to observe these students outside school, which will require further permission from parents who may be reluctant to respond.'

Experiments with Context Links to Education

The Basics

Experiments are favoured by **positivist** sociologists as they follow a **standardised** scientific structure. They allow the sociologist to measure the impact of one variable on another in a **controlled** setting, meaning that variables, other than those being measured, can be isolated. Positivists believe that by discovering laws of **cause and effect** they can reveal social facts (values, norms and causes in society which shape human behaviour).

There are two types of experiment: **field experiments** and **laboratory experiments**. Field experiments take place in the natural environment (for example, a school if studying education). Laboratory experiments take place in a controlled environment using a scientific method and allow the sociologist to have a tighter control over variables affecting participants.

Laboratory Experiments

Laboratory experiments allow sociologists to map trends and discover cause and effect relationships between variables. They create **quantitative data** which is easy to analyse; this can be presented visually in graphs and tables. Laboratory experiments follow a strict scientific procedure which is standardised, meaning a set of instructions can be created for the repetition of the experiment. This ensures laboratory experiments are **reliable**, allowing sociologists to map trends and pattern changes over time.

Laboratory experiments are often reliable and therefore allow sociologists to map trends and pattern changes over time.

EVALUATION POINT

Interpretivist sociologists disapprove of the experimental method. They believe that human behaviour is too complex to place into easily quantifiable measurements. Interpretivists would suggest that experiments **lack validity** as they fail to uncover the meanings that individuals apply to their own actions. They would argue that it is impossible to control all variables that may impact on individuals. If an object is pushed it will move as a natural result; if a human is pushed they will aim to work out why and how to respond, making measuring their responses more difficult.

Laboratory experiments take place in an **artificial environment**, far from the 'real world' which, for sociologists, they are aiming to research. Interpretivists would argue that actions that take place in the laboratory are too disconnected from those which would take place in real life situations.

Human behaviour often changes when people know that they are being studied. This phenomenon is known as the **Hawthorne effect** and clearly impacts on the validity of any findings that sociologists may uncover. In avoiding the Hawthorne effect sociologists may not disclose the true purpose of their research, which presents ethical issues as participants are being deceived.

Because of the restrictions of the laboratory, only small samples can be researched. This makes laboratory experiments lack representativeness as the sample researched is often too small to form generalisations about the population as a whole.

Field Experiments

Field experiments take place in natural settings, aiming to gather a more valid view of the 'real world' rather than behaviour that simply takes place in a laboratory. Field experiments are usually **covert**, therefore the research participants are unaware of the fact that they are being studied. In a field experiment the sociologist will construct or use existing situations which allow them to measure behaviours of participants.

One example of a field experiment is that of Rosenhan (1973) and his **'pseudo patient'** experiment. Rosenhan, along with seven others, turned up at 12 mental hospitals in California stating that they were hearing voices in their heads. Once admitted the pseudo patients were kept in the mental hospitals for an average of 19 days, despite claiming that they had stopped hearing voices as soon as they entered. Rosenhan aimed to measure the **'labels'** that people attach to individuals and their impact. He discovered that the participants' behaviour had little impact on their diagnosis of schizophrenia; instead, the diagnosis was based on the labels that were originally attached to the participants when they presented themselves to the mental hospitals in the first place.

EVALUATION POINT

Field experiments allow the sociologist less control over the variables that may impact on participants' behaviour. It is impossible to measure the impact of one variable in a natural setting, with so many potential influences in the 'field' environment. Interpretivists suggest that field experiments simply measure behaviour, rather than uncovering meanings behind the behaviours of individuals. Because of the nature of field experiments, they often prevent the sociologists from gathering informed consent from participants, which leads to **ethical issues.**

Emile Durkheim (1897) conducted a 'thought experiment', also known as the **'comparative method'.** This type of experiment simply allows the sociologist to compare two sets of data to find cause and effect relationships. Durkheim aimed to discover the causes of suicide. In comparing the suicide rates of Protestant and Catholic Christians he found that Catholics were less likely to commit suicide. Durkheim questioned the differences between Catholics and Protestants and believed Catholics to be more integrated in society. He then attributed the lower suicide rate to the higher levels of social integration.

EVALUATION POINT

The comparative method allows the researcher to map trends in statistics from events that have already taken place. This can find pattern changes over time and measure the impact of key events. It is also highly ethical as there is no deception for participants.

Experiments in the Context of Education

When researching pupils, laboratory experiments pose ethical concerns as they often have a physical or psychological impact on the participant. Due to their age pupils are a vulnerable group and this should be respected by the sociologists gathering informed consent from parents and guardians.

The laboratory is an artificial environment and will cause changes in pupil behaviour because of its difference from an educational setting. Despite this, field experiments can take place in a classroom setting. This means that the sociologist is able to research the impact of changes in variables in a natural educational setting.

One example of a field experiment which has taken place in education is that of Rosenthal and Jacobson (1968). They researched a Californian primary school administering an IQ test to pupils. An experimental group of students was selected at random from the results. Rosenthal and Jacobson suggested to the school staff that these pupils would be able to make significant progress as they would 'spurt' ahead of others. On return to the school Rosenthal and Jacobson found that because of the positive labelling of the identified group, they had made more progress than the other pupils. Through this field experiment Rosenthal and Jacobson were able to measure the impact of the self-fulfilling prophecy.

SUMMARY

- Experiments are favoured by positivist sociologists as they follow a standardised scientific structure and use quantitative data.

- Laboratory experiments take place in a controlled setting and follow a standardised procedure; as a result of this they produce reliable data.

- Interpretivists reject laboratory experiments as they believe that human behaviour is too complex to quantify. They also state that the Hawthorne effect is likely to cause findings from experiments to lack validity.

- Field experiments take place in the natural environment and are usually covert. Because of this there are ethical implications for the sociologist to consider.

- Rosenhan's 'pseudo patient' field experiment allowed him to map the impact of labels when applied to patients of mental hospitals.

- Emile Durkheim used a comparative method to map trends between social integration and suicide rates.

- Rosenthal and Jacobson used a field experiment in an educational setting to measure the impact of the self-fulfilling prophecy on primary school students.

QUICK TEST

1. Which type of sociologist favours the use of experiments?

2. Why are experiments a reliable research method?

3. What are the two main types of experiment?

4. In Rosenthal and Jacobson's field experiment, what was the main concept being measured?

5. Which key term is used to describe the phenomenon that participants are likely to change their behaviour when they know that they are taking part in an experiment?

6. Which type of experiment did Emile Durkheim use when studying suicide rates among Catholic and Protestant Christians?

7. What is meant by the term 'covert' when applied to field experiments?

8. Which sociologist studied the impact of 'labels' on 'pseudo patients'?

9. Why might field experiments be considered to gather more valid findings than laboratory experiments?

10. Why do laboratory experiments tend to lack representativeness?

PRACTICE QUESTIONS

Question 1 (AS Level style): Outline two advantages of using laboratory experiments. (4 marks) **Spend 6 minutes on your response.**

> **HINTS TO HELP YOU RESPOND**
> Start each advantage on a new line. Explain why your advantage improves the research. For example: 'Laboratory experiments take place in a controlled setting. Because of this, variables that impact on an individual's behaviour can be removed or reduced, allowing the sociologist to measure the variables that they are specifically interested in.'

> **Item A**
> Sociological research has identified that teachers label students based upon their own ideas of the 'ideal pupil'. Some students are negatively labelled and others feel the benefit of teachers judging them positively. Labels can be created by teachers according to a pupil's social class, ethnicity or gender. These labels can lead to a self-fulfilling prophecy. To obtain a high standard of response you must make direct links between the nature of the research method specifically linked to the context of education, in this case observation specifically to study anti-school subcultures. It may not be possible to make every point a direct link, though the more detailed and direct your links are the better your response will be.
>
> Experiments have been favoured by many sociologists as a means of investigating the impact of labels applied by teachers on students. Laboratory and field experiments have a range of benefits and pitfalls when used to study phenomena in education. The effectiveness of the experimental method, when applied to education is highly debated.

Question 2 (AS and A Level style): Applying material from Item A and your knowledge of research methods, evaluate the strengths and limitations of experiments for studying the impact of the self-fulfilling prophecy on pupil achievement. (20 marks) **Spend 30 minutes on your response.**

> **HINTS TO HELP YOU RESPOND**
> Start by reading through the item and finding any hooks that you can include in your response. Here you will see a number of useful pieces of information to inspire you, from the idea of the 'ideal pupil' through to that of 'social class, ethnicity and gender', as leading factors in the creation of labels by teachers. Your response must aim to make significant links between the nature of self-fulfilling prophecies and their impact on achievement and experiments.
>
> Question the practical, ethical and theoretical factors surrounding experiments and relate these to the self-fulfilling prophecy. For example: 'In measuring the impact of the self-fulfilling prophecy on a pupil experiments allow the researcher to quantify pupil achievement and find patterns between this and the labels applied to the pupil by their teacher. This is a practical advantage as results will be quick to analyse. However, there will be significant ethical implications as the sociologist is encouraging teachers to treat their pupils differently. Pupils who are labelled negatively for an experiment may end up performing badly on assessments. When a sociologist meddles in a pupil's educational achievement ethical implications will occur.'
>
> Plan accurate links between the method and the educational context. Aim to base your response around these links.

Questionnaires with Context Links to Education

Questionnaires are a form of **social survey**. They can be administered in a range of different ways: through the **post**, **face-to-face** or via **email**. Questionnaires are favoured by **positivists** as the pre-set questions that they contain usually gather **quantitative data**. Responses tend to be categorised allowing for patterns between variables to be measured easily. Questionnaires are naturally **standardised** as the same questions are in each questionnaire, which means that the method is easily repeated as all sociologists need to do is use the same questions in their repetition of the study, making questionnaires highly reliable.

Because of the nature of questionnaires they allow the researcher to study responses from large samples (that is, groups representing the population that the research is studying). By reaching vast numbers of the sampling frame, questionnaires are considered to be **representative**.

EVALUATION POINT

Interpretivists reject the use of questionnaires as they fail to gather true insightful findings. They are concerned about the lack of depth in the quantifiable responses. Interpretivists suggest that as a result of this questionnaires **lack validity** and 'verstehen' (understanding of human behaviour). Email questionnaires are easily ignored and only really completed by respondents who have time on their hands or are passionate about the subject impacting on their representativeness. Face-to-face questionnaires may cause respondents to feel uneasy, responding in a way that they feel is socially acceptable rather than speaking the truth.

Sociologists do not have to be present when questionnaires are completed, allowing them to remain **detached** from the research. This means that they are less likely to influence the respondents, allowing the research to be **objective** (without any bias) and largely unaffected by the sociologist's own opinions. Despite this the sociologist's values will still have an impact on the questions that they select to include.

EVALUATION POINT

The fixed questions that questionnaires use in their standardised approach fail to allow **flexibility** in the research. Sociologists are not able to delve deeper and ask probing questions to find out the meanings and reasons that people attach to their answers. This makes interpretivists question the validity of the method. As the sociologist is often not present during the completion of the questionnaire the respondent is often unable to clarify the meaning of questions. **Misunderstanding** caused by this can also impact on the validity of responses.

Questionnaires have a number of practical advantages. They are fairly cheap to produce and can reach a large sample quickly. Because of this they are representative. They can be **easily distributed** electronically via email. Online surveys can be easily distributed through the use of social media. Once returned the quantitative data is easy and **quick to analyse** (due to closed questions) in order to map cause and effect relationships and discover social facts.

Response rates can often be low, especially for postal questionnaires. This can be affected by the length of a questionnaire, as individuals are less likely to complete lengthy questionnaires. Sociologists may have to add incentives to respond and this can prove costly. As questionnaires have to be kept short, the range of data gathered is often restricted. Postal questionnaires are notoriously poor for gathering representative responses; certain groups in society are more likely to respond than others. Individuals who have more 'spare time' will be more likely to respond. Also, groups who value the research will be keen to influence the findings, which makes the questionnaires less representative.

As a result of the standardised procedure they follow, questionnaires are highly **reliable**. They can be easily replicated by another sociologist at a different time in order to map changes in the impact of variables over time.

When using questionnaires sociologists rarely encounter any ethical issues. Respondents are naturally providing consent in responding to the questionnaire. However, the sociologist must still ensure that they are informed of the purposes of the research. Respondents can remain **anonymous** if needed and be given the option to respond to each question or not.

As the sociologist often designs the questionnaires many questions may be misleading or aim to guide respondents to select certain answers. By choosing to include some questions over others the sociologist's thoughts and opinions may impact on the findings. Allowing respondents to remain anonymous may also mean that the sociologist is unaware as to whether or not the intended respondent completed the questionnaire.

Questionnaires in the Context of Education

Questionnaires are often used in education to gain an insight into the experiences of pupils, parents and teachers. Questionnaires are easy to distribute across schools as pupils can complete responses in class. This means that the response rate can be high among students. However, some pupils may see questionnaires as extra work expected of them and respond negatively, particularly those in **anti-school** subcultures. Parents may be harder to reach with pupils often responsible for taking the questionnaire home. Some parents are more likely to respond than others. Parents who have complaints about the education of their child may be more eager to voice their concerns. This means that sociologists may be more likely to receive negative responses and less representative findings.

Sociologists need to take care when designing questionnaires for pupils to complete. Pupils' level of **understanding** will vary across ability ranges and year groups. Often sociologists will need to simplify their questions. If questions are not simplified there is a risk that some pupils will not understand them, and responses may then lack validity.

Sociologists must gain permission from gatekeepers in school (such as the head teacher) in order to distribute their questionnaires. Due to the **marketisation** of schools they will often deny the opportunity to research if the questionnaire is likely to show them in a negative way.

Questionnaires must be carefully designed in order to gain valid responses from participants.

SUMMARY

- Questionnaires are favoured by positivists as they gather quantitative data which can be used to map trends.

- They can be conducted face-to-face, through the post or via email reaching a large sample, making them representative.

- Interpretivists reject questionnaires as they do not produce validity.

- The design of questionnaires must ensure that the respondent is able to understand the questions.

- The researcher is detached from the respondent making questionnaires objective.

- Questionnaires are quick to distribute and analyse.

- As questionnaires follow a standardised procedure they are easily repeated, making them reliable.

- Questionnaires are ethically sound as respondents can easily opt out and also remain anonymous.

- In education samples are easy to obtain and so make responses representative, though responses may vary due to attitudes towards schools.

QUICK TEST

1. Which type of sociologist favours questionnaires?

2. Why must sociologists take care when designing the questions in their research?

3. Name two ways in which questionnaires can be conducted.

4. Questionnaires follow a standardised procedure with set questions and pre-coded responses. How does this make them reliable?

5. Which group of students are likely to view a questionnaire as unnecessary work and therefore fail to respond?

6. Why would schools be reluctant to allow questionnaires to take place that may show them in a negative way?

7. What type of data do questionnaires mainly gather?

8. Why do interpretivists reject the use of questionnaires?

9. Which key term describes a research method which is unbiased and allows the sociologist to remain detached from the research?

10. Which parents may be more eager to respond to questionnaires about schools?

PRACTICE QUESTIONS

Question 1 (AS Level style): Evaluate the strengths of using postal questionnaires. (16 marks) **Spend 25 minutes on your response.**

HINTS TO HELP YOU RESPOND

Make sure you are specifically discussing questionnaires that have been posted to respondents. Outline the practical strengths of being quick to distribute through the postal system and then also to analyse. Evaluate this using the likelihood of a poor response rate from certain groups. Explain that questionnaires are ethically sound as the respondent has the option as to whether or not they complete the questionnaire. Discuss the reliability and objectivity of the questionnaire, explaining how a standardised procedure is used with set questions and the researcher is detached from the research. Evaluate this by using the problem that a lack of face-to-face contact means that the researcher is not able to explain the questions, causing some misunderstanding and impacting on the validity of the postal questionnaire. Continue to explain strengths and seek out supporting or contrasting points in order to evaluate them. Use effective connectives between your points, such as, 'in contrast to this' or 'critiquing this' to show that you are evaluating.

Question 2 (A Level style): Outline and explain two ways in which Interpretivists reject questionnaires. (10 marks) **Spend 15 minutes on your response.**

HINTS TO HELP YOU RESPOND

Here two detailed PEEL paragraphs are needed (make a point, evidence it, explain it and link it to the question). You can focus on issues which impact on validity as this is the main aim of an Interpretivist. Points you could discuss are the lack of ability to clarify the meaning of questions with the sociologist, impacting on a respondent's understanding and how this leads to confused responses that lack validity. You may choose to focus on the sociologist being detached from the research and how they are unable to probe or delve deeper into responses to find the true causes of the response.

Observation with Context Links to Education

Interpretivists favour the use of observation to study society as it produces **valid** findings and allows them to uncover the meanings that individuals attach to their actions. Observation allows the sociologist to witness the actions of participants first hand, seeing real behaviour in its **natural setting**. There are a number of different types of observation, each with its own advantages and disadvantages.

Observing pupils in the classroom can allow sociologists to gain an insight into behaviour in its natural setting.

Participant observation involves the researcher taking part in the event that they are observing by becoming part of the group themselves. **Non-participant observation** allows the researcher to watch the event without taking part. **Overt** observation is when the researcher's identity and purpose is known to the participants. Some **positivists** may use this alongside structured recording sheets in order to generate statistics on what is being observed. **Covert** observation involves the researcher remaining 'under cover' with their identity and true cause unknown to the group being researched.

Recording of behaviour can be difficult during observation. **Structured observation** allows the researcher to classify the behaviours that they witness into categories, making it easy to analyse. **Unstructured observation** is much more free as the researcher simply records what they have observed using any means available.

Participant observation can produce really valid data as the sociologist is able to experience first-hand the events which they are observing, often as part of the group themselves. Observing groups in their natural settings provides an **authentic** view of their behaviour. This authenticity increases with covert observation as the researcher's identity and aims are not known by the participants – as a result they should act more naturally.

EVALUATION POINT

Gaining access to a group to observe may be difficult. Participants may be wary of **outsiders** or people who are new to their social group, and they may be concerned about revealing their true thoughts and actions as a result. True trust of a group can only be gained over time, causing practical issues for the sociologist. The group's behaviour may change, even if the study is covert.

Covert research can be considered **unethical** as it breaches the need for informed consent which is a prerequisite for ethical research. Participants are deceived by the researcher and must be **debriefed** about the study in order to overcome this. It may also be very difficult when researching criminal or deviant groups.

Throughout participant observation the sociologist is able to work freely around their hypothesis, moving with the research group to focus specifically on areas that interest them. They are able to adapt their hypothesis and also delve deeper to gather a more valid image of the meanings that individuals attach to their behaviours. Participant observation allows the sociologist **insight** into the experiences of the group that they are observing. As part of the group themselves they may be more empathetic to the causes of behaviour that they observe.

Regular movement of a fixed hypothesis can mean that research lacks focus. Sociologists conducting participant observation are likely to develop a strong **rapport** (relationship of understanding) with the group they are observing, which can have an impact on the sociologist's ability to remain objective and detach their own opinions and feelings from the research itself. Sociologists are at risk of 'going **native**' which means to become part of the group they are studying, impacting on the validity of the findings of their research and the ethics of the study. Participant observation is difficult with large samples; therefore it lacks representativeness. The sociologist must also interpret the meanings of the actions that they observe which makes the research subjective to their own opinions. In contrast, through being subjective sociologists are able to develop an empathetic understanding (verstehen) of the sample they are observing.

Overt observation does not have the ethical implications that covert observation can have. Here participants are aware of the sociologist and their purpose. This avoids any **deception** and also allows for practical advantages such as ensuring that the sociologists can freely take written notes of behaviour while they are observing, something that cannot often happen in covert research.

When participants are aware that they are being researched they are likely to change their behaviour. This is known as the '**Hawthorne effect**'. Sociologists taking notes may cause the individuals being observed to become concerned about their own actions, and to change their behaviour as a result. This makes overt observation less valid than covert observation.

Positivists rarely use observation. When used, they prefer structured observation where observations are categorised and coded so that they can be turned into quantitative data. While using structured observation the sociologist needs to note findings regularly, which means that the research usually needs to be overt.

Different sociologists may have conflicting opinions of which behaviours fit into which categories. This makes the method less reliable as the same sociologist would need to repeat the observation. When noting observations the sociologist may influence the behaviour of the sample as they will clearly see which behaviours are being recorded by the sociologist, causing the Hawthorne effect to occur.

Observation in the Context of Education

Interactions that take place in education are often in **closed settings** such as the classroom. Access to the classroom is controlled by a number of **gatekeepers,** from the head teacher to the school governors. Once a sociologist has access to observe pupils and teachers they may struggle to gather valid findings. As teachers are used to being observed they are likely to change their day to day behaviour to impress the observer. Pupils may also change their behaviour as they see the researcher as an **authority figure** in the classroom. Pupils from anti-school subcultures may act up, aiming to show their teacher and school in a negative way.

Permission from parents is not needed when sociologists have gained access to observe normal school behaviour. This means that observation in schools has practical advantages. Despite this, observation in classrooms is still limited in terms of representativeness. With only around 30 students in each lesson sociologists would have to observe behaviour across a wide range of classes to make findings representative.

Observation of processes outside the classroom can prove difficult. Many of the factors impacting on pupils' achievement come from external sources. Sociologists would struggle to observe behaviour outside school and in the homes of pupils as gaining access would be an issue. Covert and participant approaches are likely not to be possible in school settings.

SUMMARY

- Interpretivists favour observation as the insight that it allows provides valid data. It mainly focuses on qualitative data which gathers meanings behind an individual's actions.

- Observation comes in a variety of forms: participant, non-participant, covert, overt, structured and unstructured.

- Covert observation is high in validity as it does not cause the Hawthorne effect. It can, however, be considered unethical with participants possibly being deceived.

- Participant observation allows the researcher a true insight into the behaviours of those observed. Bonds with the group may cause the sociologist to go native impacting on validity.

- Overt observation avoids deception and provides practical advantages when note taking.

- Positivists rarely use observation. If they do they use structured observation with observations categorised into quantitative data.

- Observation in an educational setting tends to involve small samples which impacts on the representativeness of findings. Students and teachers may experience the Hawthorne effect when being observed.

QUICK TEST

1. What is the difference between 'covert' and 'overt' observation?

2. Positivists rarely use observation; when they do what type do they use and why?

3. Why does participant observation provide insight for the sociologist?

4. Which key term describes the action of changing behaviours when participants are aware that they are being observed?

5. Which key ethical implication does overt observation avoid?

6. Why might observation be considered to lack representativeness?

7. What is meant by the term to 'go native'?

8. Why might pupils from an anti-school subculture change their behaviour if they are aware they are being observed?

9. Name two 'gatekeepers' who may control access for sociologists wishing to observe in schools.

10. Why is it difficult to categorise behaviour using structured observation?

PRACTICE QUESTIONS

Item A

Many sociologists are interested in the impact of classroom interactions on working class pupils' achievement in school. They often suggest that the actions that take place within the classroom are a key factor in causing a class gap in achievement between middle class and working class pupils. Sociologists have found that teachers are likely to label working class students negatively as they fail to meet the teacher's view of the 'ideal pupil'. This causes the pupil to experience a self-fulfilling prophecy.

Sociologists may use observation to study classroom interactions and their impact on working class students. By observing classroom behaviour first-hand they are able to gather an insight into the internal causes of the class gap in achievement.

Question 1 (AS and A Level style): Applying material from Item A and your knowledge of research methods, evaluate the strengths and limitations of non-participant observation to study the impact of classroom interactions on working class underachievement. (20 marks) **Spend 30 minutes on your response.**

HINTS TO HELP YOU RESPOND

You must specifically apply your knowledge of how effective non-participant observation is for studying the impact of classroom interactions on working class pupils. You should start by reading the item and looking for any key hooks that you have not already considered and put these into your plan. Look for direct links between the method and the context. They can be strengths or weaknesses, for example, non-participant observation often lacks validity when used to study the impact of classroom interactions on working class pupils. This is because teachers will be reluctant to show any biased behaviour while they are being observed. The Hawthorne effect will mean that working class pupils, who may normally be labelled as underachievers, are treated equally in the group, with teacher time being balanced across each pupil regardless of social class.'

Offer contrast between your points by using effective connectives that show you are linking your points into a chain of reasoning. When you have mentioned one point use another that links to it and always aim to link back to the question in order to ensure that your response is focused.

Question 2 (AS Level style): Outline two reasons why sociologists may choose to use covert observation. (4 marks) **Spend 6 minutes on your response.**

HINTS TO HELP YOU RESPOND

Two bullet points are sufficient in response to this question. You can use the view that remaining covert adds validity to the research. You could also discuss the idea that covert research means that the sociologist does not have to spend time gathering informed consent.

Interviews with Context Links to Education

There are many different types of interview used by sociologists. **Positivists** favour **structured interviews** which are often called 'formal' interviews and take the format of a questionnaire conducted either **face-to-face** or over the **phone**. Structured interviews use fixed questions which are delivered in the same way to each interviewee; this is called an **'interview schedule'**. The questions asked require closed responses which provide **quantitative** data. This data can then be used to map trends and discover cause and effect relationships between variables.

Face-to-face interviews can provide sociologists with the information they need to be able to map data trends.

As structured interviews follow a **standardised procedure** they are easily repeated by different researchers, making them highly **reliable**. This also means that numerous researchers can administer the structured interview, gathering data from a large sample making structured interviews **representative**. Respondents are also more likely to take part as the interviewer is present and can explain the importance of the interview. As a result of the convenience of fixed questions, structured interviews do not require much time and are therefore cost effective. They can also be carried out by researchers who do not require intensive training.

EVALUATION POINT

Structured interviews do not allow for detailed responses and interviewees are limited in their choice of responses. This means that the findings often lack validity as sociologists are not able to delve deeper for an understanding of why interviewees respond in the way that they do.

Interpretivists reject the use of structured interviews as they fail to gather qualitative data. Interpretivists focus on validity as the main aim of their research as opposed to the reliability and representativeness that structured interviews gain.

Considering that structured interviews simply allow the sociologist to ask the same questions again and again, they are not cost effective in comparison to questionnaires which provide similar findings. By asking **fixed questions** the sociologist is not able to develop a rapport with the interviewee, which can cause issues around sensitive topics, making interviewees reluctant to share opinions and experiences.

Interpretivists prefer the use of unstructured interviews which gather qualitative data and allow for more valid findings. Unstructured interviews ask **open-ended questions** and allow the sociologist to be flexible with their questioning, using the format of a guided conversation with a focus around a certain topic. Unstructured interviews encourage more detailed and varied responses, obtaining more depth and therefore more validity in their findings.

Unstructured interviews allow the sociologist to gather information about the meanings that individuals attach to their actions. They are better than structured interviews at researching more sensitive issues as the sociologist is able to adapt their questions to suit the situation. As unstructured interviews are less formal, the sociologist is able to build a **rapport** with the interviewee. Positive relationships based on a strong rapport are more likely to produce truthful findings as the interviewee is comfortable in sharing honest and open thoughts with the interviewer.

When using unstructured interviews sociologists can often research a group of interviewees. By interviewing a group of people at one time the sociologist is able to save time and gather a more representative sample. Group interviews allow interviewees to share ideas and remind each other of key information, and as a result they gather a vast wealth of information.

EVALUATION POINT

Positivists believe that unstructured interviews are an ineffective method for the study of society as they fail to obtain their main goal of **reliability**. As questions in unstructured interviews encourage varied and detailed responses they produce less reliable findings. The responses are qualitative and as a result difficult to analyse, requiring more time to evaluate.

Unstructured interviews take longer to complete; therefore only small samples can be used in order for research to be cost effective, making the method lack **representativeness**. Interviewees may opt out of the unstructured interview if the topic area is a sensitive subject. They may feel uncomfortable discussing sensitive issues face-to-face.

The rapport that is gained between interviewer and interviewee in unstructured interviews can also, at times, impact on the validity of the findings. The subjective nature of the interview can mean that interviewees respond in different ways to different interviewers. Interviewees may feel that they should give responses that the interviewer wants to hear. This is known as the **'interviewer effect'**, responding in a way that they believe to be 'socially desirable'.

In group interviews interviewees may feel pressure to respond in a way that pleases other members of the group, meaning that individual opinions are not heard.

Interviews in the Context of Education

Interviewing pupils in education can prove difficult at times as young people often struggle to develop clear, coherent answers because of their differing levels of understanding across age groups and abilities. Some pupils may use a **restricted language code** and have limited vocabulary, which may limit the meaningfulness of responses and, in turn, impact on the validity of the research.

Pupils may be reluctant to respond to an adult interviewer as they may see them as an **authority figure** (much like a teacher). This may make pupils change their responses as a result of the interviewer effect.

Sociologists may have to obtain **informed consent** from a number of sources, from head teachers, teachers, governors or parents. Gatekeepers may be reluctant to allow sociologists to conduct interviews in schools as they may disrupt the learning of pupils.

In group interviews pupils are likely to experience **peer pressure** to respond in a way that reflects the opinions of the group rather than themselves as an individual. Pupils are strongly influenced by their peers. This can, however, be a benefit to the researcher as dynamics within the group can also be researched. Pupils in anti-school subcultures may encourage each other to 'act up' in interviews in order to disrupt the research.

DAY 5

SUMMARY

- Positivists favour structured interviews as they follow a standardised procedure and allow for their main goal of reliability.
- Structured interviews follow a standardised procedure and require fixed responses from fixed questions called an 'interview schedule'.
- Structured interviews allow for large numbers of people to be interviewed and are therefore more likely to be representative.
- Interpretivists use unstructured interviews to discover valid findings. They used open-ended questions to gain detailed responses.
- Unstructured interviews allow the sociologist to develop a rapport with the interviewee, which can ensure more truthful answers.
- Interviewees may respond untruthfully in order to give responses that they feel are 'socially desirable'; this can impact on the validity of the interview.
- Pressure to respond in a way that is pleasing to the interviewer is known as the 'interviewer effect'.
- Pupil responses to interviews may vary as a result of different levels of understanding. Many students will respond using a restricted language code.
- Pupils may see the researcher as an authority figure and respond negatively. They may also experience peer pressure throughout group interviews.

QUICK TEST

1. Name two formats that a structured interview can take.
2. What term is given to describe a positive relationship gained between the interviewer and interviewee?
3. What type of questions do unstructured interviews ask?
4. Which type of sociologist prefers the use of structured interviews?
5. Why might pupils be reluctant to respond truthfully to an interviewer?
6. What makes unstructured interviews more likely to be unrepresentative?
7. Which type of interview is likely to be reliable as a result of its standardised procedure?
8. What term is used to describe an interviewee's pressure to respond in a way that pleases the interviewer and is seen as socially desirable?
9. Which type of interview allows interviewees to share ideas and 'bounce' ideas off each other?
10. Which group of students are likely to 'act up' in an interview situation?

PRACTICE QUESTIONS

Question 1 (A Level style): Outline and explain two advantages of unstructured interviews. (10 marks)
Spend 15 minutes on your response.

> **HINTS TO HELP YOU RESPOND**
> Here you need two detailed PEEL paragraphs (make a point, evidence it, explain it and link your point back to the question). You can mention any of the advantages, such as: ability to be valid, development of rapport or the ability to delve deeper and add questions to discover more detail. For example: 'Unstructured interviews are favoured by Interpretivist sociologists as they aim to gather valid findings. The findings from unstructured interviews are more likely to be valid as the sociologist (interviewer) is able to develop a rapport with the interviewee. This rapport will mean that the interviewee is likely to be truthful as they have a level of trust in the sociologist. This is clearly an advantage as the more detailed the findings are the more valid they become. However, this level of trust may mean that the interviewee simply responds in a way that they know pleases the interviewer. The interviewer effect will mean that the results lack validity.'

Question 2 (AS Level style): Outline two problems of using unstructured interviews. (4 marks) **Spend 6 minutes on your response.**

> **HINTS TO HELP YOU RESPOND**
> Two quick bullet points will suffice for this response. Two sentences for each can secure the 4 marks. For example: 'Unstructured interviews use open-ended questions. As a result they have varied and detailed responses which are hard to analyse.'

Question 3 (AS Level style): Outline two advantages of group interviews. (4 marks) **Spend 6 minutes on your response.**

> **HINTS TO HELP YOU RESPOND**
> Again, two bullet points will suffice here. Select any two advantages. For example: 'Group interviews allow a more representative sample to be used. They do this as they allow more interviewees to be studied at once, creating further time for more interviews to take place.'

Secondary Sources with Context Links to Education

Research by sociologists does not always use primary data (findings that have been gathered by the sociologist for the purpose of the study itself). Secondary sources make use of resources and findings that already exist. These include **documents** and **official statistics**.

Documents

Documents come in two forms. **Personal documents** include personal notes, diary entries, autobiographies, photographs, notes of memories, etc. **Public documents** include official reports which detail information from governments, businesses, etc. **Interpretivists** favour the use of documents as they are rich in **qualitative data** that can be used to discover the meanings behind actions for individuals.

Public documents are useful as they are often easy to obtain due to legal requirements enforcing their ready availability in order to be scrutinised. They are also usually free to access.

EVALUATION POINT

Public documents are often subjective as the creators of the document are aware that they will be in the **public domain**. As a result of this they will be eager to present information that shows the company or business in a positive way, omitting any negative information.

Personal documents are high in validity as they are usually detailed and give a real insight into people's views and opinions. Personal documents are already created and therefore save the sociologist time.

EVALUATION POINT

Personal documents are hard to analyse as they do not follow a standardised structure. As they are unique to individuals and events they lack reliability. Personal documents can be highly subjective as they often only represent the views of the individual who created them. They may also be aimed at a specific audience, making them difficult to understand for others. Different researchers may also interpret private and public documents in different ways, impacting on their reliability.

Historical documents are useful when researching past events. They allow sociologists to discover opinions and values of individuals who are no longer alive.

EVALUATION POINT

Historical documents may be difficult to analyse as they contain language that has changed over years. They may also be hard to obtain or even missing. It may also be unclear as to how they were put together, e.g. statistical sources, and how the figures were calculated originally may differ greatly to modern methods of gathering statistics.

Documents are often evaluated using **'content analysis'**. This is when sociologists (usually interpretivists) measure the amount of space dedicated within a document (or piece of media) to specific topics. This allows qualitative documents to be quantified, and is best used when evaluating media documents or news bulletins.

Official Statistics

Positivists like the use of official statistics as they are naturally **quantitative data** which meets their main goal of being reliable and representative. Official statistics can be **'hard statistics'** which cannot easily be disputed, such as the birth or death rate. They can also be **'soft statistics'** which can be manipulated by the researcher (and those who produce them); these include crime statistics.

Official statistics are useful as they are easy to obtain and already exist, which means that sociologists don't have to use valuable time creating them. Official statistics are often generated by **government agencies** through vast projects which question large parts of society. By using large samples official statistics are highly representative. At times people are legally required to submit information for these statistics. An example of this is the census, compiled to discover information about the population of England and Wales. The findings of this are published by the **Office for National Statistics** (ONS).

As official statistics are often generated by the government, Marxists suggest that they simply reflect the findings that they want to display. Statistics can be easily manipulated by those in power to hide areas of concern.

Official statistics can prove to be a useful starting point for further research. Trends and patterns shown in statistics can lead sociologists to look at the causes of these patterns. Sociologists may use **'triangulation'** in order to look deeper into the causes of patterns. This is when a sociologist will make use of both quantitative and qualitative methods in their research.

Secondary Sources in Education

Official statistics are readily available within the education system. Statistics which closely analyse school and pupil performance can be compared across ethnic groups, genders, social classes (through looking at which students are eligible for free school meals) and local areas. Patterns are already monitored closely by government agencies and published in **league tables** and **Ofsted reports**.

As a result of **marketisation**, school performance is easy to examine with schools forced to be transparent about pupil achievements in order for parents to compare them. This can, however, mean that schools, in order to impress prospective parents, select results to promote and display which show them positively.

Schools have their own independent way of recording incidents. This means that documents used across schools often vary and are therefore less reliable to sociologists. Schools do, however, share documents such as the **National Curriculum** which has a direct impact on a wide range of schools. Access to documents may be difficult at times as they may contain information that is sensitive and confidential, such as pupil background information.

SUMMARY

- Secondary sources already exist and can be used by sociologists to save time creating their own data.

- Personal documents include diaries, autobiographies, photos and notes of memories.

- Public documents include reports from governments and businesses.

- Interpretivists favour documents as they can be high in qualitative data.

- Historical documents allow sociologists to examine past events.

- Documents are often evaluated by using 'content analysis' in order to measure the focus areas of the document.

- Positivists like official statistics as the quantitative data can be used to map trends and find patterns of cause and effect relationships.

- Hard statistics cannot easily be disputed. Soft statistics are easily manipulated by the researcher.

- Official statistics are highly reliable. At times it is a legal requirement to provide information to be included in official statistics, such as in the census.

- Interpretivists suggest that official statistics are simply social constructs and are not as reliable as positivists believe them to be.

QUICK TEST

1. Why do secondary sources save time for the sociologist in their research?

2. What is meant by the 'dark figure of crime'?

3. Which type of document includes diary entries and photographs?

4. What type of data do official statistics contain?

5. Why is the birth rate considered to be a 'hard statistic'?

6. Suggest one document that is shared across many schools.

7. Which key term describes sociologists' use of both qualitative and quantitative research methods?

8. Why might public documents about companies and businesses omit negative information?

9. Which term is used to describe the process of measuring the amount of space given to certain topics within a document?

10. Interpretivists suggest that official statistics are 'social constructs'. What does this mean?

PRACTICE QUESTIONS

Question 1 (AS Level style): Outline two theoretical advantages of using official statistics. (4 marks) **Spend 6 minutes on your response.**

> **HINTS TO HELP YOU RESPOND**
>
> Remember the main two theoretical approaches that apply to research methods are positivism and interpretivism. Positivists would favour official statistics as they are quantitative and provide their main goals of reliability and representativeness. Two quick bullet points comprising two sentences each will suffice. For example: 'Positivists favour official statistics as they are highly reliable. They provide reliable results as they are often obtained year on year by government agencies.'

Question 2 (AS Level style): Evaluate the practical and theoretical disadvantages encountered when using documents in sociological research. (16 marks) **Spend 25 minutes on your response.**

> **HINTS TO HELP YOU RESPOND**
>
> Discuss the practical issues of obtaining some documents, and contrast this with the fact that many public documents are readily available and published by agencies such as the ONS. Mention the practical advantages of historical documents and the ease of studying the past. Contrast this with the availability of relevant historical documents which focus on the needs of the sociologist.
>
> Use the theoretical advantages of high levels of rich qualitative data and how this is the main goal of interpretivist sociologists. Evidence the depth and truthfulness of personal documents, and contrast this with the notion that they are often interpreted differently by other sociologists and are not always relevant to the research topic. Argue against the validity of public documents as a result of their aim to provide positive information about the businesses and agencies that they represent.
>
> Plan your response so that it shows a clear pattern of thought. Explain advantages and then contrast them with a connected disadvantage. Use connectives such as 'in contrast to this' or 'despite this'.

Question 3 (A Level style): Outline and explain two theoretical problems sociologists may face when using official statistics. (10 marks) **Spend 15 minutes on your response.**

> **HINTS TO HELP YOU RESPOND**
>
> Two detailed PEEL paragraphs are needed here (make your point, evidence it, explain it and link it back to the question). You can use any issues relating to official statistics that cause interpretivists to reject them. For example: 'Interpretivists reject the use of official statistics as they consider them to lack validity. Many official statistics fail to gain a true picture of the event that they aim to examine as they lack detail. Official statistics are simply a snapshot of a situation at one given time. Despite the advantage that they show cause and effect relationships, they fail to gather the true causes behind the trend. Interpretivists believe that qualitative methods are needed to show the true meanings behind individuals' actions and therefore official statistics lack validity.'

Families: Couples

Biologically Determined Roles

Talcott Parsons, a functionalist, identified two roles that men and women are biologically determined to perform. Men are naturally suited to the **instrumental role** of paid work, of being the breadwinner. Women fulfil the **expressive role**. They nurture and care for the rest of the family – they are the homemaker. These roles benefit each member of the family and wider society.

EVALUATION POINT

Feminists would argue that these roles benefit men, not wider society. Diana Leonard argued that women are socialised to a particular idea of femininity which means they accept the disadvantages of motherhood that the role brings: unpaid domestic labour, less time to themselves. The New Right support the idea of biologically determined roles and believe that these roles are complementary, bring stability and allow the family and society to prosper.

The Symmetrical Family

This is a family or couple who have shared domestic roles. Both will be in paid jobs. The couple share childcare, taking care of the house and share leisure activities. Symmetrical relationships have joint **conjugal** roles; in the past men and women were restricted to segregated conjugal roles, the separate roles of homemaker and breadwinner.

Young and Willmott (1973) saw the rise of joint conjugal roles as part of a growing trend towards more **egalitarian** or equal families, a move from extended families to **privatised nuclear families**, isolated and independent from extended kin and neighbours, and understanding the lives of TV characters more than those of the people who live in their neighbourhood. Important social changes affect couples' roles; the changing position of women in society allows them jobs which gives them greater economic power; better housing and improved living standards mean men are more home-centred. The **commercialisation of housework** means couples can buy in goods and services that ease the burden of housework. Silver and Schor argued for the **death of the housewife role** because in a wealthier society goods and services are purchased, meaning the role of homemaker is not as essential. Also, technologies such as dishwashers mean we do not have to have a life of work as a housewife. New technologies also encourage the role of the 'new man' (he does what was traditionally called 'women's work') and this further undermines the traditional 'housewife' role.

EVALUATION POINT

The feminist sociologist Ann Oakley found no evidence for 'symmetry' in her studies and was adamant that industrialisation brought about the **birth of the housewife role** when paid work was taken out of cottages/homes and placed into factories, meaning women were eventually excluded from the factories and worked unpaid at home as housewives. This shows the housewife role is not natural but a **social construct** – that is, created by a particular society or culture.

The March of Progress

The idea that equality between couples is growing is known as a **March of Progress** view. It is seen as a progressive step forward for families with evidence of women working seen as directly leading to a more equal division of unpaid labour between couples (Gershuny 1994). Gershuny believed that **lagged adaptation** means that in time seeing their fathers doing 'women's' tasks and having greater symmetry will lead to men taking on more of the household tasks as 'natural'. Whereas women adjust readily to their new role as wage earner, men lag behind in adjusting.

Mary Boulton argued that men help in enjoyable tasks but are not responsible for demanding childcare. She found less than one in five husbands had a significant role in looking after children. This could be because **gender-role socialisation** means jobs in and out of the home are sex-typed (men do the DIY, women do the cooking). Men have internalised asymmetrical norms.

Feminist Views – Evidence against the March of Progress or Symmetry

Women being in work has led to a **dual burden** of unpaid housework and a paid job. Ferri and Smith (1996) found women in paid work did not lessen their responsibility for childcare. The reason for this, argue feminists, is that society is **patriarchal**. This means men hold power and authority over women, they have a privileged position which they will not give up as they benefit from their power. Some sociologists argue that as soon as women start to earn the same rewards for paid work as men society will become less patriarchal. Other sociologists see that powerful cultural forces, such as gender-role socialisation, reinforce inequality through the **ideology of motherhood**. Hochschild (1983) found that women, far more than men, could be found in jobs that necessitated 'emotional labour' – caring for sick people or teaching. This led to claims by Duncombe and Marsden (1995) that women performed a **triple shift** of housework and paid work and **'emotion work'**, that is, work that is done in caring for the emotions or mental wellbeing of the family.

Man Yee Kan found women being in paid work resulted in men doing more 'women's' work than their fathers. She recognised poorer women are still subjected to oppression by the family because of the dual burden or triple shift. Gillian Dunne, a radical feminist, found that lesbian couples were more likely to be in a position to reject the **gender-role script** that they were socialised to because they can negotiate roles between themselves and their partners. This supports the idea that heterosexual couples are socialised to certain roles and men feel that their masculinity is challenged when adapting to a greater share of housework; norms have been deeply internalised.

Who Controls the Resources and Who Makes the Decisions?

Research into who makes the decisions in families by Edgell (1980) and repeated by Hardill (1997) found that men had the final say on the most important decisions, e.g. buying a house. Couples shared decisions on holidays and children's schooling, with small decisions about daily shopping being left to women. This hierarchy of decision making can be used as proof that men have more power in society. Kempson (1994) has shown that women put the other family members' needs before their own when resources are scarce. This can lead to women being impoverished. Pahl and Vogler (1993) identified two ways in which finances are organised in families. The traditional allowance system gives more power to men because housewives are given a budget or allowance with which to manage the family finances. Dual wage earning couples show, increasingly, pooling of financial responsibilities, through joint bank accounts, allowing spending to be equally shared by husband and wife.

SUMMARY

- Many sociologists see factors such as gender equality, a rise in living standards, women working and new technologies in the home creating greater symmetry between couples.

- The commercialisation of housework has resulted in the death of the housewife role.

- With the rise of the 'new man' and women working, couples have experienced a March of Progress – women and men are equal in work and in the home.

- Evidence from feminist sociologists shows that women are not equal but carry a dual burden of paid work and unpaid household work.

- Duncombe and Marsden suggested that women perform a triple shift of housework and paid work and emotion work.

- Gillian Dunne argued that heterosexual couples find it difficult to break free of their gender-role scripts; these are the identities that men and women are socialised to from birth. They prevent men and women from adapting to equal roles.

- Men still make the important decisions in the family and have control over finances. This is changing for symmetrical couples who pool resources.

QUICK TEST

1. Which key terms did Young and Willmott use to describe couples that share housework and domestic chores?

2. Why do functionalists and the New Right support the idea of biologically determined roles?

3. What is meant by the commercialisation of housework?

4. What does Oakley mean by the 'birth of the housewife role'?

5. Which key term is used to describe both the paid job and the unpaid domestic chores women do?

6. What is meant by the 'expressive' role?

7. Identify three reasons for more equal relationships between couples.

8. What is meant by 'emotion work'?

9. State one major criticism of the March of Progress view of relationships between couples.

10. Why would a heterosexual male feel 'threatened' by doing a more equal share of housework?

PRACTICE QUESTIONS

Item A

March of Progress sociologists would argue that couples share domestic labour more equally now than in the past. Functionalists argue that equal but different roles are naturally played by men and women.

On the other hand, some feminist writers find evidence that women still do most of the household chores, while also having paid jobs, and are excluded from important decision making. If they challenge their husbands' power they are subjected to abuse.

Question 1 (AS and A Level style): Applying material from Item A, evaluate the view that there has been a March of Progress with women and men sharing symmetrical roles today. (20 marks) **Spend 30 minutes on your response.**

HINTS TO HELP YOU RESPOND

In this response you are asked to 'evaluate'. This means looking at the advantages and disadvantages of the argument. You will note that the core debate within your essay here is about whether or not the relationship between couples has become more equal. You must first state clearly what the March of Progress view includes and give supporting evidence for it. Show the weaknesses of each point in the argument as made by sociologists arguing for improvement in the position of women. Your response must naturally link between points to form a chain of reasoning. For example, discuss how Young and Willmott suggested that a woman being in paid work has led to more equal relationships, then evaluate with evidence from feminist sociologists of the inequalities of, for example, the dual burden carried by women. Between your points use connectives which show you are evaluating, such as 'in contrast to this' or 'supporting this theory'. You may conclude that women have achieved a greater equality but still do not have complete equality of power within relationships.

Item B

Despite the fact that women are protected by the Equality Act 2010 from discrimination in all areas of life, equality of work opportunities have not brought about equality of domestic unpaid labour. Women, according to radical feminists, are exploited within the family. Many other sociologists would argue that women have greater choices than ever before with maternity rights and divorce laws allowing women a greater input into decision making between couples.

Question 2 (A Level style): Applying material from Item B, analyse two ways in which women could be viewed as exploited within families today. (10 marks) **Spend 15 minutes on your response.**

HINTS TO HELP YOU RESPOND

The item has suggested areas of concern about how women are still exploited, for example 'unpaid domestic labour'. From this point you could analyse the dual burden and the triple shift that cause women to invest more time than men in unpaid housework and thus be exploited. In analysing, discuss each point and explain it, then question it, using an opposing viewpoint. For example, you may discuss the 'dual burden' but use the idea of the 'new man' to suggest men are responding to an awareness of women's exploitation. Your second change can be to do with decision making and the continued patriarchal structure of the household. Men still have final say in the important financial decisions. Choose only two and 'unpack' these concepts or ideas in detail.

Childhood

Childhood is not a natural state. Childhood is not fixed. Experiences of childhood vary from culture to culture, place to place or from time to time. Childhood can be summed up as being a subjective rather than an objective experience. It is a **social construct** – created (constructed) depending on the kind of society (culture) a person experiences. Stephen Wagg supported the view that childhood is a social construct, while at the same time recognising that each person undergoes the same stages of development biologically: infant, child, youth, adult.

The 'Western' Notion of Childhood

An examination of the 'western' notion of childhood will show that there is no single 'natural' state of childhood. As Philippe Ariès' book *Centuries of Childhood* (1960) confirmed, childhood is a shifting concept and not universal. Ariès had the idea that the modern 'western' notion of childhood as innocent and vulnerable and in need of protection emerged as the community gave way to the family in the 17th century; eventually, in the 19th century we get established the modern day **'cult of childhood'**. Societies of this type regard children as entitled to happiness (Cunningham 2007), with access to the resources of society providing a **separate** (Pilcher 1995), protected environment safe from the dangers of the adult world. In the medieval period children were seen as mini-adults after the age of seven years. Medieval art showed children had no separate culture of their own. Paintings depicted young people participating in adult games and adult work and they did not have different clothing from adults. The power of the church helped change this view of children as little adults. The innocent and corruptible nature of children of God was emphasised with priests put in charge of educating children in Cathedral schools. Also, Ariès believed attachments to children grew more sentimental as the infant mortality rate fell. Edward Shorter concluded that parents were distant and remote from their children in the Middle Ages because of the high death rates of children.

The March of Progress

The growing numbers of children being educated by an increasingly powerful church changed the view of children from indifference to watchful control. This, along with the greater personal and financial investment in children because of falling death rates, created the conditions for improved lives among young people. Guidebooks for parenting of children arose at a time of growing affluence among the middle classes; specific clothing emerged to accompany the biological stages of development of a child. Laws banning child labour, welfare legislation protecting children from harm or cruelty, legislation to prevent children engaging in sexual activity before age 16 or smoking imposed the idea that different behaviour was expected of children. Eventually, there emerged a child-centred society, one in which the conditions for children were much improved from the past, without fear of death, assault or exploitation.

EVALUATION POINT

Some sociologists argue against the idea of a March of Progress, pointing to differences between class, gender and ethnicity that affect childhood experience. Girls are subjected to greater controls over their behaviour than boys, Mayer Hillman (1993) found that boys were given fewer restrictions over cycling, crossing roads and being out after dark on their own. Poorer children have fewer opportunities academically. Lareau's research supported the idea that childhood is socially constructed and tied to social class. Often wealthier parents will direct their children to activities that benefit them socially: music, dance and outdoor leisure. Working class parents were only concerned with health, safety and love.

Conflict Views of Childhood

Gittins (1998) has argued that rather than a golden age of childhood being found in modern western society, there is growing domination and control of children by adults – this is known as **age patriarchy**. Children's lives are controlled to such an extent that they lack the freedoms and powers of the past. Four key areas of control are: *space* – adults control the areas children can access; *time* – when a child rises or sleeps or eats; *bodies* – what they wear; and *money* – pocket money or employment laws that prevent children working (economic).

EVALUATION POINT

Hockey and James (1993) argued that children acting up and acting down are ways that they resist adult authority and control, for example by drinking or smoking (acting up) or by wanting to be carried (acting down). Firestone (1979) is a **child liberationist** seeing the protections that adults offer children as new forms of oppression from which children need freeing; a good example of this is denying children the ability to earn money through paid employment. However, the Children's Act 1989 allows children protections and gives parents responsibilities towards children and is a sign that children are not subject to age patriarchy.

Childhood is disappearing at a 'dazzling speed' argued Neil Postman (1994). In an age where print culture has been replaced by television culture children have instant access to adult themes: death, sex and violence. In the age of print culture these adult themes had been inaccessible to children, as skills to access these themes (literacy) were essential, so a separate stage of childhood emerged. Now that **information hierarchy** has been destroyed. Children need no extensive period of education to access the adult world; it is being given to them with the rise of TV culture, and they aspire to the same clothing, games and culture. Laws give children the same rights as adults. The innocent protected period of childhood has gone as children have free access to information that encourages a worldly cynicism.

EVALUATION POINT

According to Opie and Opie (1993) a separate childhood still exists. They found that children created their own games and culture. Their research was based on observation over many decades and contradicts Postman's view that fewer and fewer children play unsupervised games.

Toxic Childhood

According to Sue Palmer (2009) children's mental and physical health has been damaged by a cultural and technological transformation. With parents working more hours, children have more unsupervised time in front of computers or television screens. This makes them vulnerable to marketing campaigns and contributes to a culture of consuming over intellectual curiosity. Children are targeted as a market for unhealthy foods that contribute to obesity. Continuous testing in schools adds to the 'toxic' mix of influences that poison the experience of childhood today.

EVALUATION POINT

Giddens (1992) argued that families are becoming more democratic in their relationships as intimacy increases within families. This postmodern influenced idea regards respect as being earned by all family members and not given unquestioningly. Punch (2002) argued that a whole different set of expectations is applied to the children in non-western cultures. They are asked to take responsibility at an early age and contribute through work to the community.

DAY 5

SUMMARY

- The experience of childhood is not fixed but subjective and is socially constructed.
- Ariès demonstrated childhood is not a universal experience, rather it emerged because of historical, economic and cultural factors.
- The factors include the industrial revolution, which transformed society creating wealth and giving more time for parents to be with family. A declining infant mortality rate and laws to regulate children and protect them along with compulsory schooling established the 'western' notion of childhood.
- The March of Progress view of childhood sees childhood as greatly improved from the past. Laws protect children and the family offers love and security.
- Child liberationists see the increased protection as age patriarchy – adult power and control over children from which children need freeing.
- Childhood is disappearing because children now have access to the adult themes of death, sex and violence that the information hierarchy shielded them from before the arrival of television culture.
- A toxic childhood awaits children in western societies today: little parental contact time, subjected to junk food diets, exposed to too much testing and television.

QUICK TEST

1. Which sociologist looked into the development of the 'cult of childhood'?
2. What do sociologists mean when they argue that childhood is a 'social construct'?
3. What, according to Shorter, was the main reason adults were 'distant and remote' towards children in the Middle Ages?
4. Which key phrase is used to describe the theory that childhood has improved from the past to the present?
5. List three factors that encouraged a 'golden age of childhood' to develop.
6. What is the term given to the process by which adults have power and control over children?
7. What do wealthier parents do for their children that may be different to working class parents?
8. Which sociologist studied the impact of the 'information hierarchy' on childhood?
9. According to Hockey and James how do children resist adult power and authority?
10. Which theorist argued that childhood is now 'toxic'?

PRACTICE QUESTIONS

Item A

There is statistical evidence to suggest childhood can be a period of neglect and abuse. Rather than being a place of security and protection, children are still vulnerable within society and can become victims of domestic violence from siblings. Beyond this children feel depressed and anxious with media portraying sexualised images of children that distort body image. A recent UNICEF survey on children's wellbeing ranked the United Kingdom 16th out of 29.

Others will point to the fact that 90% of the low weight births are in developing countries and that the United Kingdom has good levels of literacy and numeracy.

Question 1 (AS and A Level style): Applying material from Item A and your knowledge, evaluate the view that childhood today is 'disappearing'. (20 marks) **Spend 30 minutes on your response.**

HINTS TO HELP YOU RESPOND

In this response you are asked to 'evaluate'. This means looking at the advantages and disadvantages of the argument. You will note that the core debate within your essay here is about whether or not childhood is disappearing. You will evaluate this idea against the fact that childhood has only recently been socially constructed as a separate time. Discuss how, according to Neil Postman, childhood has come under threat from the rise of television culture and the factors leading to the rise and fall of the information hierarchy. You can contrast this view with those of the March of Progress sociologists who believe that childhood is improving. Key concepts such as age patriarchy will allow you to develop your essay displaying your knowledge of how childhood is socially constructed and not universal. Remember to show how even within a society childhood experience can vary greatly based on class, gender and ethnicity. You may conclude that rather than childhood 'disappearing', the way we socially construct childhood is changing and some see children as more or less vulnerable based on their theoretical view.

Item B

According to one source a child will cost parents £227 000 by the time that child reaches 21 years of age. Parents are spending more time with their children and parents give huge amounts emotionally to their children. Some postmodern thinkers believe we live in an age of greater personal choice and freedom, with children given greater say in the family now than in the past. Others see children as victims of commercialisation, identified as consumers and marketed at. Many sociologists look back at the past and see childhood as a 'nightmare from which we are now awakening'.

Question 2 (A Level style): Applying material from Item B analyse two changes in the way we socially construct childhood over the past 100 years. (10 marks) **Spend 15 minutes on your response.**

HINTS TO HELP YOU RESPOND

To reach the highest marks evaluate the points you identify. If you argue that children have greater freedom to choose for themselves you can argue against this by identifying that childhood may have become toxic as children are targeted as consumers or indeed that childhood is disappearing. Or perhaps they are subjected to more control today through the school day, testing and parental fears over stranger danger. The last line of the item is pointing out the March of Progress view of childhood and so you can make this one of your points to explain; give examples of and argue against.

Families: Functionalist Perspective on the Family

The functionalist view of the family is a **structural** theory. This means that functionalism develops from the view that institutions can and do shape individuals. Functionalism is a **consensus theory** that sees the role of the family being to work with other institutions to help socialise society's members to a set of agreed norms and values. In this way the family works for the benefit of each individual and all members of society. To illustrate this idea a comparison is made between society and the human body. The **organic analogy** states that the wellbeing of the body is dependent on the correct functioning of each organ of the body. The vital organs perform vital functions, necessary for the wellbeing of the body. Just as the heart oxygenates the body, the nuclear family performs essential functions for society.

The heterosexual monogamous nuclear family is viewed as universal (this means found everywhere) and essential for the wellbeing of society. Without the nuclear family society would not function cooperatively as the values and the norms of society would not be correctly socialised to new generations. This would lead to a breakdown in the proper functioning of society.

George Peter Murdock (1949) studied 250 societies across the planet and identified **four essential functions** that the family performs. These functions are why the monogamous heterosexual nuclear family is universal – found in all societies: 1 Stable satisfaction of the sex drive prevents a 'sexual free-for-all' that is divisive and ruinous to communities. 2 Reproduces the next generation otherwise there is no 'society'. 3 Socialisation of the next generation to the shared norms and values of society (the **value consensus**). 4 Meeting the economic needs of society such as sustenance and shelter through the gendered roles each contributes in a complementary fashion.

EVALUATION POINT

Not everyone benefits equally from the family. Conflict theorists would dispute the consensus view, pointing to the exploitation of both women and children within families as evidence that society is based on conflict not consensus. For feminists the source of the conflict is gender based and the family serves the needs of men by exploiting women. For Marxists the exploitation is class based with the capitalist class that owns the means of production (factories) exploiting all others in society for their own enrichment (see pages 88–89).

Two Irreducible Functions of the Family

Talcott Parsons (1955) a prominent functionalist theorist developed the idea of the **functional 'fit'** in relation to the role of families in different types of society. In our industrialised societies the functions of the family had been reduced to two functions that other institutions within society were incapable of performing in place of the family. Stabilisation of adult personalities and the primary socialisation of the young were the **two irreducible functions**. Other agencies could provide health or social care for members but only the family could perform these two functions so that stable, healthy societies continued.

In pre-industrial communities, which were smaller and based more on farming, the need for supportive extended families, for example cousins and grandparents, was much more immediately felt with people living off the land and working together in their cottages. Families were a **unit of production**; they defended themselves in times of conflict and looked after each other when ill. After industrialisation people moved from tight-knit, unchanging, predominantly agricultural communities to larger town and city populations where a nuclear family was best suited to the demands of an industrialised economy. To be able to follow the available jobs in mills and factories, which were built to accommodate the large machinery of a new industrial era, families were better able to be geographically mobile if they were nuclear in structure. Parsons argued that this is why the nuclear family develops; it is easier to move to follow work if the family has two generations and not three (so-called geographical mobility). Also, because the nuclear family has less extended kin networks the barriers to social mobility are less. Pressures to follow family traditions are less. With the relative isolation that being in a nuclear family brought a person did not have to be limited to their 'inherited' social position (**ascribed status**) but could seek to advance themselves beyond their own status in a world that was seeking to reward achievement. Achieved status better suited the new specialised industrial manufacturing base of the economy.

EVALUATION POINT

There is a huge amount of evidence to contradict the idea that pre-industrial societies were better suited by the extended family and that industrialised societies are best suited by the nuclear family. Willmott and Young found that in migrating to urban environments people relied on kin to support each other through hardships. Michael Anderson's (1971) study of Preston showed precisely this; extended kin lived together to combat poverty or unemployment during industrialisation. Willmott and Young showed that before industrialisation cottage industries were based on the nuclear family not the extended family. Each family in each cottage would work, as parents and children, not extended kin, to produce products. More importantly, the historian Peter Laslett (1972) found from records on pre-industrial England (1564–1821) that only one in every ten households was extended. Many examples of extended family forms exist today giving support to the wider family by supplying help with looking after children, money to overcome financial obstacles and advice.

Ronald Fletcher – The Family is Gaining Functions

The British functionalist Ronald Fletcher argued that the family is gaining functions as we now have the time and finances to care more about the members of our family; the family is important as a **unit of consumption** – spending to boost economic activity. We put a lot of time, energy and money into raising our children, getting children into the right nurseries, schools and activities. For Fletcher, the institutions that Parsons argued have replaced the family, such as the NHS, support families in their roles as carers and do not replace that function of the family. In the past, Fletcher argued, people were so burdened by the need to survive that the health of livestock would be more important than the health of the family. With people living longer and increased wealth there is a greater emphasis on companionship rather than economic necessity between couples.

In the way that a **warm bath** relaxes the body and soothes the mind the family can support the individual by creating a safe space for each person to be himself or herself or act in a childish fashion. This is similar to the idea of the stabilisation of adult personalities in that both Fletcher and Parsons were suggesting the family has a beneficial role to play in supporting people to be healthy functioning members of society.

EVALUATION POINT

Fletcher has a 'March of Progress' view of the family that is slightly different to other functionalist viewpoints. He noted that the 'privatised' family was not interested in the problems of society because it had become somewhat isolated from society. Marxists also see the family as a warm bath or safe haven, a place of retreat from the oppressive and exploitative world of capitalism. The frustrations built up from the work environment can be unloaded in the privacy of the home, where the exploited worker relaxes and complains about work, without challenging the true source of that oppression and unhappiness – the boss. Do not get the two views confused – there are some similarities but huge differences.

SUMMARY

- Functionalism is a structural theory that believes in a value consensus.

- George Murdock believed that the family was universal and essential.

- Murdock identified the four essential functions of the family to be: stabilise the sex drive, reproduce the next generation, socialise the next generation, economic provision through the division of labour.

- Talcott Parsons identified a functional fit: extended families fit pre-industrial societies and nuclear families fit industrialised societies.

- Parsons thought that the nuclear family fits industrial societies because it is small and it allows for social mobility in a time when people with the best skills to fit the job should be awarded the job.

- Parsons argued that the functions of the family have been reduced in industrial societies; the two irreducible functions are stabilisation of adult personalities and socialisation of the young.

- Ronald Fletcher argued that the functions of the family have been extended and changed to roles such as companionship between couples. The economic function is as a unit of consumption and the investments of time and money in the welfare of children by parents are much greater than in the past.

- In the warm bath theory, the family provides a place for adults to be themselves away from the stress and pressure of adult life.

QUICK TEST

1. Which sociologist argued that the family is universal and essential?

2. What is the organic analogy?

3. What are the four essential functions of the family?

4. What term is given to the idea that the family socialises children to the agreed norms and values of wider society?

5. What did Talcott Parsons mean by a functional 'fit'?

6. What term is given to the process by which a person's social status is fixed by birth?

7. Functionalists argue that families are no longer a 'unit of production'; what does that mean?

8. What two irreducible functions does the family perform?

9. What two criticisms of the idea of a functional 'fit' can be identified?

10. Give two functions that Fletcher believed the family has gained since industrialisation.

PRACTICE QUESTIONS

Question 1 (AS Level style): Outline and explain two advantages of the functional 'fit' theory suggested by functionalist Talcott Parsons. (10 marks) **Spend 15 minutes on your response.**

HINTS TO HELP YOU RESPOND

You must explain two advantages of the theory. In your first paragraph you can identify that it provides a link between the need for a geographically mobile workforce and the dominance of nuclear families within modern industrialised economies. Be sure that you do some analysis of the theory. For example, suggest that historical research has undermined the idea that nuclear families did not dominate in pre-industrial England. The second paragraph must address a distinctly different point such as the nuclear family provides for greater social mobility. The detail comes from explaining key ideas about ascribed status and the need within industrialised economies for workers with specialised skill sets, thus promoting those people benefits society. Promotion of younger more able members of society may cause conflict in extended families where the head of the family would feel threatened by a younger family member with greater social status because of their career success. Your writing needs be detailed and you would write between 150 and 250 words.

Item A

Some sociologists insist that stabilising adult personalities and socialising the young are the key roles that families perform today. Since we now live in urban environments in modern states there is no need to be self-sufficient in regards to production of resources, health care and education.

For other sociologists agencies outside the household merely support the family in providing care and love to their offspring.

Question 2 (AS and A Level style): Applying material from Item A and your knowledge, evaluate the view that the contemporary family is losing its functions. (20 marks) **Spend 30 minutes on your response.**

HINTS TO HELP YOU RESPOND

Structure your response so that each paragraph addresses a key point about the functionalist views of the family. This question seems so difficult but really it is quite simple. Different functionalists have differing views on the family. Contemporary simply means today, so always be keen to expand your vocabulary to be able to fully understand what the question is asking. You just have to relate your knowledge of functionalist views a step at a time. So you can start with Murdock and his views on the essential functions of the family. Compare those views to Parsons' idea of a functional 'fit' and the irreducible functions of the family. Identify those functions and write about the functions the family no longer performs according to Parsons. To evaluate Parsons you can use Fletcher and argue that he regards the family as having gained functions. Your evaluation will also benefit from examining feminist ideas of the family having retained functions as a unit of production through free domestic labour provided by women or a reserve army of labour according to Marxist feminists. Address the question directly at the end of every paragraph and come to a separate conclusion.

Families: The Marxist Perspective on the Family

Marxism is a **conflict perspective** and a structural theory, meaning that it is based on examining conflict between groups within society and understanding how these structures or the institutions of society shape individual identity and therefore shape society. The economic base of society determines all the other relations within society and that relationship is one of exploitation of the majority of people by a minority who own the **means of production** (land, factories). Just as education is a means of perpetuating social or class inequality and **capitalism**, so too is the family an important institution in perpetuating inequalities in society and supporting capitalism. Capitalism has been explained on pages 8–9.

Friedrich Engels – *The Origin of the Family, Private Property and the State* (1902)

Marx had identified a form of society called **primitive communism**. People did not have property but owned knowledge, tools and skills collectively unlike a capitalist economic system that relies on the private ownership of the means of production. In *The Origin of the Family, Private Property and the State*, Engels described the development of monogamous families to support the development of capitalism. To be able to pass on the means of production from one father to his legitimate heir, monogamous relationships had to be secured. In 'primitive' societies there was no **monogamy** (one man and woman faithful and exclusive to each other in their sexual relationship) but rather what Engels described as the **promiscuous horde** from which it was difficult to distinguish legitimate heirs. As farming techniques developed wealth accumulation followed, and that wealth needed passing on to the legitimate heir. This is why capitalism encouraged monogamous nuclear families: what Engels described as 'the world historical

defeat for the female sex' as women became 'mere instruments for the production of children'. Just as the proletariat were oppressed and dominated by the bourgeoisie, men dominated their wives assisted by the law and religious obligations.

EVALUATION POINT

The evidence to support Engels' ideas is uncertain. The Marxist explanation does not explain the diversity of family forms that exist in modern capitalist societies. However, at the time of writing there was no evidence or knowledge of such diversity of family forms. Engels himself acknowledged that women from proletarian backgrounds had the chance to work in industry but that women from bourgeois backgrounds were denied this choice. A woman's economic situation necessitated her entering into the exploitative economic relationship with the bourgeoisie. Functionalists would argue that the theory depends too much on the analysis of the economic relationships. The family performs beneficial functions for society such as socialising the young to the value consensus and securing stability for the individual and wider community.

Eli Zaretsky – *Capitalism, the Family and Personal Life* (1976)

Zaretsky makes it clear that the real objective of the family is to produce obedient workers for an unequal and exploitative capitalist economic system. There is no desire for stabilising and socialising for the betterment of all members of society as Parsons insisted.

The family teaches deference to authority, just as work within the unfair capitalist system requires uncritical obedience. We learn to respect our elders in families, just as we respect the 'boss' who would be the source of our unhappiness. The family teaches us acceptance of inequality as if inequality were the natural state of relationships. The proletariat may think that perhaps working harder would bring more personal success and reward rather than examining the conditions of their own exploitation. This is how the proletariat mind is shaped to accepting the capitalist worldview. This is the ideological function of the family. It is suggested that a man with family responsibilities would be less likely to take strike action against unfair working practices. The family is also said to offer a haven from the alienating world of work. The factory processes create a world of work tensions that can only be relieved by the privatised home where sanctuary is sought among the same cheap domestic goods that the workers make. This haven is not only a distraction from the harsh realities of capitalism but also the key engine for capitalism's growth in the sale of consumer goods to families. Families become enamoured of designer goods and modern devices for the decoration of the privatised home, and the young become socialised to a world of 'false needs'.

Marxist Feminism

Marxist Feminist	Key Idea
Margaret Benston	The male breadwinner is made efficient to capitalism by having women perform unpaid domestic labour. She ensures his conformity because he supports her and cannot think about strike action, as the family would suffer. She raises the future workforce to serve capitalism.
Fran Ansley	Workers are prevented from venting their anger about their pay and conditions of work by having the family on which to vent their anger about their alienation (they cannot see a point to what they produce) from work.
Veronica Beechey	Women are a reserve army of labour. They do not have power because they have no secure work. They fill in when there are shortages of workers and are dismissed readily when capitalism does not need them. This prevents women organising effectively to protect their rights.
Heidi Hartmann	Patriarchy is essential in explaining the position of women within the exploitative capitalist system. Women are exploited twice: by capitalism and by male power and control.

EVALUATION POINT

The benefits of capitalism may outweigh the perceived evils, with a higher standard of living being available to people. Is the family a negative experience? Maybe individuals gain from emotional support and financial stability within families. Marxism as a structural theory tends to treat all families as the same nuclear type. Families may resist capitalist ideology and consumer values and socialise their children to Marxist ideas. The point is it treats all families as victims when they may be resisting or cooperating with capitalism out of a clear choice to do so.

EVALUATION POINT

The Marxist view of the family offers a more detailed view of the development of the family. Critics believe that Marxist feminists do not take account of those women who are in work out of choice and benefit from the family through companionship, love and security. There are other types of family other than the monogamous nuclear family with biologically determined gender roles.

SUMMARY

- The family is a key institution in the continuation of an exploitative capitalist system.

- Friedrich Engels argued that the need to secure the inherited wealth of the bourgeoisie led to the encouragement of the monogamous nuclear family, where a father's rightful son and heir could be identified.

- Eli Zaretsky showed the family to be a key factor in the continuing dominance of capitalism as it has an ideological role of socialising society's members to inequality by showing the system to be fair and unalterable.

- Individuals are socialised to be obedient workers within this system by learning to defer to authority.

- Zaretsky also showed the family to be a key unit of consumption. The workers make the goods and the families are encouraged by, for example, the media to buy goods to adorn their bodies and fill up their homes.

- Marxist feminists see women as doubly exploited by capitalism and patriarchal power, serving the needs of capitalism and men by caring for them and rearing the next generation of workers. Women absorb the anger of alienated men in the supposedly 'safe' haven of their homes.

QUICK TEST

1. Why was the promiscuous horde replaced by monogamous marriage?

2. Which author described the ideological functions of the family?

3. Give two examples of the ideological functioning of the family.

4. Name two ways in which the family home can be a 'sanctuary' away from the world of work.

5. Explain how the family becomes an important unit of consumption for the success of capitalism as an economic system.

6. What key benefit may critics of Marxist theory suggest is provided by living under a capitalist economy?

7. Which member of the family is responsible for the raising of the future labour force of capitalism?

8. According to Fran Ansley, what prevents male workers taking action against the exploitative capitalist system?

9. Which sociologist argued that women act as a reserve army of labour for the capitalist economy?

10. According to Marxist feminists, how are women exploited 'twice' within society?

PRACTICE QUESTIONS

Item A
Sociologists have argued that the family benefits all members of society. Marxist sociologists do not agree and argue that the family serves the interests of a particular economic system called capitalism. Feminists assert that the family oppresses women and subordinates women to male power.

Question 1 (AS and A Level style): Applying material from Item A and your knowledge, evaluate the Marxist perspective on the family. (20 marks) **Spend 30 minutes on your response.**

HINTS TO HELP YOU RESPOND

This question is simply asking you about the strengths and weaknesses of the Marxist analysis of the family. You need to look at each function that Marxists see the family as serving and outline that function specifically; then look at the strengths and weaknesses of each point. Start by outlining the core beliefs of Marxism and its complex view of the functions of the family. You can do this chronologically as presented above. Evaluation points give you lots of chance to show your knowledge of other views of the function of the family in contrast to or support of the Marxist view. You can be critical of these other views in that they may not have the complex analysis that Marxist analyses provide or may ignore the problems that family life contains. You can place special emphasis on Marxist feminists to evaluate Marxist views of the family.

Use Item A to help you; expand on key points to show your own knowledge. For example, in the first line of the item it is simple to point out that functionalists believe the family benefits everyone and is a consensus theory. This leaves you free to contrast with the conflict perspective of Marxism, and identify the source of the conflict. Now you are using the detailed vocabulary of sociology. Remember your conclusion must weigh up the contribution that Marxist ideas have to our understanding of the family within modern society. Potentially it can explain consumerism, patterns of violence and powerlessness or subservience among women and children and inequality more generally, so there are plenty of key ideas to evaluate.

Question 2 (AS Level style): Outline **three** reasons why the family may be seen to contribute to inequality. (6 marks) **Spend 9 minutes on your response.**

HINTS TO HELP YOU RESPOND

This type of question can be answered in bullet points. Two marks are given for clearly outlining an appropriate reason.

The question is not directly asking for Marxist explanations of social class inequality but this is the objective of the question. Simply stating Zaretsky's ideas and explaining each one or illustrating with an example will get you the full marks. For example: 'The family teaches us to defer to authority figures so that we become obedient workers in an exploitative system.'

Families: Feminist Perspectives on the Family

Feminists see the family as socialising the young to gender roles that are vastly unequal. The inequality serves the interests of men within the family and society more generally. Women are socialised to provide free domestic labour through childcare and housework that benefits heterosexual males. Feminism is a **conflict perspective**, the source of conflict being the oppression of women by men in society through: low expectations of women beyond their role as homemakers; presenting women in stereotypical roles that continue their domestic oppression; women being subordinate when it comes to decision making in the household; roles within families being based on the misguided idea of a natural biological suitability to perform those roles. All of these ideas are challenged by feminists and can be concisely summed up by feminists' opposition to **patriarchal** societies. **Patriarchy** is the domination and control of women by men.

equality between the sexes. Liberal feminists would highlight the changes to employment laws, the provision of childcare facilities and the rise of the 'new man' as examples of a movement towards greater equality. *The Feminine Mystique* written by Betty Friedan (1963) was critical of how women are limited by the expectations of motherhood and femininity to roles that exclude them from academic opportunities or careers. For liberal feminists many of the barriers to equality have now been removed and women are not prisoners of the **feminine mystique**, a set of attitudes that constrain women to be contented with the roles of housewife and mother. Friedan's focus on founding the National Organisation for Women (1966) was to gain equality of opportunity for women in a 'man's world'. The language of sexism, stereotyping and lack of opportunity for women can be seen by liberal feminists to have been successfully challenged – they point to the March of Progress.

EVALUATION POINT

The New Right have a political view that emphasises the 'natural' division of labour into complementary but different roles. They argue that questioning gender-role socialisation as a set of 'outside forces' rather than a process that reinforces natural roles is dangerous to the stability and health of societies. From this perspective feminist arguments are absurd and a threat to the stability of society through the undermining of heterosexual monogamous nuclear families.

EVALUATION POINT

Ann Oakley (1973) identified how boys and girls were socialised to very different gender roles through a process she called 'canalisation'; boys were encouraged to play with toys that encouraged them to build and be adventurers in the world, whereas girls were encouraged to be 'pretty girls' who played house and played quietly, withdrawn from the world of adventure and 'doing'. For many feminists these processes are still present in the socialisation of stereotypical gender roles for boys and girls and are the basis on which males still dominate in society, reducing women to subordinate roles of mother and housewife.

Liberal Feminism

Liberal feminists are close to the idea of 'March of Progress' sociologists. Following on from the first wave of feminists in the 19th century, they are sometimes called second wave feminists. They believe that with changes to the law society can make progress towards

Radical Feminism

Women's exploitation will not end with changes to legislation. This is because the **patriarchal monogamous nuclear family** is to blame for gender inequality. Women are oppressed and controlled by patriarchal ideology that serves the interests of all men through the exploitation of all women. To build true equality between the sexes, to liberate women from patriarchal oppression the family would have to be abolished as it exists now. Shulamith Firestone (1970) gave some points of guidance on what should happen for patriarchy to disappear: test-tube babies would free women from patriarchy; marriage and families would be abolished; households (between seven and ten adults) would apply for licences to raise children; all older children and adults would be carers, thus eliminating matriarchal and patriarchal figures.

EVALUATION POINT

Many women would disagree that monogamous heterosexual relationships are exploitative. Women can find mutual respect, comfort, companionship and equality within these relationships; these are benefits that functionalists would highlight. Radical feminists have been criticised for ignoring the voices of women who value the childrearing role, the carer role, the expressive role as important and significant within society. Firestone's ideas have been regarded as problematic, ignoring the feminisation of the economy and, according to Hakim (1995), refusing to acknowledge women making rational choices that lead to traditional nuclear family structures.

Domestic violence occurs because the family is a patriarchal institution. When a man feels his dominance is being challenged violence occurs. Delphy and Leonard (1992) highlighted the benefits that accrue to men from the inequalities that exist because of a patriarchal ideology that puts unequal amounts of work on women in comparison to men. The homemaker and breadwinner roles legitimise partner violence against women. Official statistics show that more than a quarter of women are victims of domestic abuse – more than double the number of male victims. Abuse can be physical, sexual, stalking, emotional and financial. Dobash and Dobash (1979) argued that marriage reinforces patriarchy and thus domestic violence. Their husbands regarded women as possessions so when relationships were ended men, with no previous history of violence, reacted violently.

Some radical and Marxist feminists advocate living apart from men completely (separatism) as the only solution to men who are aggressive, competitive and seek to dominate. They would point to the underreporting of violence, the viewing of the family as something good and a private sphere not to be meddled in as obstacles to improving conditions for women in society.

EVALUATION POINT

Liberal feminists would point to the new legislation the government introduced in 2015 that prevents 'coercive and controlling behaviour' by a partner as an argument against separatism. **Separatism** (that is, living apart from men completely to solve the problem of aggressive, competitive and domineering male characteristics) is a key outcome for **Marxist feminists** (see pages 88–89). They would point to the underreporting of violence (men occupy the important positions in the police and courts), the viewing of the family as something good and a private sphere not to be meddled in as obstacles to improving conditions for women in society. Richard Wilkinson found that **social inequality** was the root cause of domestic violence as it put stress on relationships. It was not only women who suffered violence but also people in rented accommodation, low income families and children and young people were more likely to suffer.

Difference feminists argue that past arguments were dominated by a mainly white middle class version of women's oppressions. **Difference feminism** describes the different issues that feminists may focus on. For some black women the family can be seen as a source of support and resistance to racism. Ecofeminism addresses the environment and women's issues. Not all women will focus on the same issues as Christianity and goddess worship, for example.

SUMMARY

- Feminism is a conflict perspective and focuses on the most important source of that conflict in society.
- Patriarchal ideology is the idea that men are breadwinners and women homemakers and men are more highly valued for their role as breadwinners.
- Patriarchy literally means 'rule by the father' or male domination and control of women.
- Liberal feminists believe that progress has been made to a more equal balance of power between men and women in society.
- Radical feminists argue that inequality between men and women is not ended by changes to the law.
- The patriarchal monogamous nuclear family is the source of the continued exploitation of women in society – it has to be abolished for exploitation to end.
- Evidence for this is violence against women – the homemaker and breadwinner roles legitimise partner violence against women.
- Social inequality is the root cause of domestic violence, according to Richard Wilkinson.
- Difference feminism describes the different issues that feminists may focus on.

QUICK TEST

1. What is meant by 'roles within families being based on the misguided idea of a natural biological suitability to perform those roles'?
2. Why do the New Right believe that feminist ideas are 'absurd' and 'wrong'?
3. State three pieces of evidence used to support liberal feminist ideas.
4. What is meant by the term 'feminine mystique'?
5. What did Ann Oakley mean by the term 'canalisation'?
6. Give three ways in which structures need to change in order for families to disappear according to Shulamith Firestone.
7. What was the cause of domestic violence in the view of Rebecca Dobash and Russell Dobash?
8. What would 'separatism' involve?
9. Why would some radical and Marxist feminists see separatism as the only solution to inequality caused by patriarchy?
10. What is 'difference feminism'?

PRACTICE QUESTIONS

Item A
According to Faludi women still perform 70% of domestic labour. This is alongside having a career. If women have been liberated from the housewife role there are many pressures that may make women want to return to that role. Many sociologists believe that there is still a long way to go before women are the equals of men in society and that the negative image of feminism is reproduced to resist changes that would disempower men. Others would argue that feminism has achieved the aims it set out with and further changes would bring instability to the family and society.

Question 1 (AS and A Level style): Applying material from Item A and your knowledge, evaluate the contribution of feminist sociologists to an understanding of family roles and relationships. (20 marks) **Spend 30 minutes on your response.**

HINTS TO HELP YOU RESPOND
In this response you are asked to 'evaluate'. This means looking at the advantages and disadvantages of the argument. The majority of your essay should focus on the core understandings that feminism has brought to our knowledge of both the **roles** and **relationships** within families. Of course, the key issue is the socialisation of all the family to a patriarchal ideology. Your response must consider the range of feminist ideas. For example, discuss the ideas of liberal feminists in contrast to radical feminists. Marxist feminism has a different but complementary form of conflict to analyse so include that. Your evaluation must include New Right and functionalist criticisms of the feminist analysis of roles and relationships; you can also outline their contrasting understanding of the family. The conclusion will sustain and summarise the main body of the essay. Obviously it has contributed enormously because the effects can be seen in laws made to create a fairer society, e.g. the Equal Pay Act.

Item B
Families encourage the gender-role socialisation of both girls and boys. The instrumental role of the father and the expressive role often played by the mother are too strongly adhered to by nuclear families for children not to become socialised to these roles themselves. The biological suitability of women to the caring role is used to put excessive demands on women, leaving them trapped and fearful of male violence if they resist the decisions made by men within the family. This is the dark side of the family, where violence and abuse are hidden from view by the private sphere of idealised family life.

Question 2 (A Level style): Applying material from Item B, analyse two ways in which the traditional nuclear family supports patriarchal ideology. (10 marks) **Spend 15 minutes on your response.**

HINTS TO HELP YOU RESPOND
You must use two points from the item. Study the item carefully, annotate it in the examination so you can clearly see your two points. You will note that the item mentions 'gender-role socialisation'; this could be linked to 'canalisation' and evaluated through the ideas of liberal feminists and the concept of 'feminine mystique'. Secondly, resistance to the decisions of men and domestic violence can be highlighted as a means of ensuring patriarchal ideology is continued. Evaluate this idea with Richard Wilkinson's ideas about the victims being from many categories, not just women.

Personal Life Views of the Family

This view is influenced by postmodern research into culture and identity and by **interactionist** ideas. The fundamental ideas of this theory concern personal choice. An individual makes **active choices** about the relationships they form just as, postmodernists believe, a person actively constructs their own identity, like a shopper choosing from a range of consumer goods. The personal life view looks at the meanings each individual gives to the 'family' relationships that they have and choose to have. This is often contrasted with functionalist or Marxist views of the family in which individual relationships are determined by the structures that already exist. Functionalist and Marxist analysis focuses on the traditional nuclear family, leaving much to be explored in an age of diverse family types.

The diverse types of relationships which people define as 'family' include, for example, **fictive kin**. These are close friends who are regarded as family, such as when children call the close friend of their father 'uncle'. Pets are also thought of as part of the family, according to Becky Tipper (2011).

Pets are often regarded as part of the family.

Friends may have closer relationships with each other than with brothers or sisters. People actively construct their own familial bonds. This is especially true in **chosen families** that include fictive kin,

friends or indeed anyone that is part of a network of relationships selected for the support they give to a person. Chosen families is a term that has been applied to gay or lesbian families as homosexuals were subject to rejection by their own 'kin' and sought out support from within friendships and the gay community. Interactionists have also examined the relationships the living have with dead relatives, as the **memory of dead relatives** may guide the actions of the living.

EVALUATION POINT

Functionalists would argue that the focus of this broad definition of what constitutes a family is so wide-ranging as to be useless in the practical analysis of families and households. In broadening the focus the personal life view ignores the key elements of significance that make the traditional nuclear family so critical for the harmony and wellbeing of individuals and society. There are also arguments that suggest discounting the significance of blood ties people have is turning away from an essential truth about how humans form relationships through marriage and value their kin. To counter this the personal life view should not seek to ignore relationships based on marriage or on blood ties. The proponents of this view argue that they seek to ask individuals how they value those relationships and others.

Carol Smart (2007) investigated the meanings that gay and lesbian couples gave to the control of finances within the relationship. It is thought that the person who makes the final decisions in a relationship has more power and the person controlling the money is the one who has the final say. Smart found this not to always be the case in the gay and lesbian couples she interviewed. No meaning was given to who controlled the money. One partner did not feel inferior or less equal because they had no control of the money. In fact, from taking into account the personal life views of gay and lesbian couples, sociologists have uncovered useful information about how gender-role socialisation plays a significant part in heterosexual relationships. Same-sex couples have greater room for negotiation or flexibility in sharing responsibilities for a wide range of living arrangements. Carol Smart found that same-sex couples may pool some of their finances but keep money for themselves to spend as they wish, free from socialised gender-role expectations or norms.

The personal life perspective has also been used to criticise the **individualisation thesis** that states people are completely free to define their own roles within relationships. Vanessa May called the view 'idealised' because it makes judgements that exclude class, ethnicity or how connected the individual is to others through intimacy, emotion, economics and social dependency. This justifies the personal life view examining past relationships as they are not forgotten but form a dense weave that forms the fabric of familial relationships.

Family life views have been critical in establishing new areas of research for the sociology of childhood. Berry Mayall has criticised the analysis of the social construction of childhood as being **adultist**. Adults have drawn conclusions from their own viewpoint about the experiences that are significant in defining 'childhood' without investigating the stories of children themselves. Children are not 'projects' but are active in creating and defining what it means to be a child. It has been found that children are not just acted on by the decisions made by the adults in their household or family. They contribute to finding solutions to family problems and they are active, not passive (see pages 80–81).

EVALUATION POINT

Child liberationists, who seek to free children from what they regard as excessive control and power that is exercised over them, favour the new sociology of childhood that derives from the theoretical stance of the personal life view.

EVALUATION POINT

Anthony Giddens would argue that the individual's role overshadows the roles of the state, the church or any other structures such as social class or ethnicity. This is rejected by the family life perspective because if research finds out that ethnicity has had a major impact on shaping the decisions about relationships then that structure is far from a fading influence on their lives.

The structures may be so strong as to influence people's lives in a negative way. Patriarchy is an obvious example. The Houses of Parliament is still male dominated, men still make decisions in the traditional nuclear family. Women may suffer abuse because of a challenge to a man's power or authority. In a subtler but still obvious form Anna Einarsdottir (2011) cited the idea of **heteronormativity** (pressure to conform to heterosexual lifestyles or norms), coercing lesbian women who have careers into remaining in the closet. A woman is allowed to operate in roles that would have been thought masculine in the past but they must retain their femininity as symbolised or defined by their heterosexuality.

SUMMARY

- Family life perspectives are derived from postmodern theories about individual choice but do not ignore structures completely.

- The view is linked to interactionism and is the opposite of functionalist or Marxist views which see the structures imposing all the conditions of family relationships.

- Fictive kin are friends that are viewed as family.

- Chosen families is a term often associated with gay and lesbian families that have exercised greater choice in creating a supportive network of relationships.

- Family life view is critical of the individualisation thesis; people are not entirely free to make choices but have to negotiate relationships because of emotional bonds, a sense of belonging and the care they have for others.

- The family life view has been successfully used to trace the diversity of family types, the relationships of gay couples and to shed light on new ways to investigate 'childhood'.

QUICK TEST

1. State two theories that the 'family life view' is associated with.

2. Define 'fictive kin'.

3. Define 'chosen families'.

4. Which sociologist suggested that pets were regarded as family members?

5. According to functionalists the family life view is not useful for investigating families. Why?

6. Give two ways in which the individualisation thesis ignores the persistence of structures as an influence in an individual's life.

7. Which sociologist argued that the structures are less important than personal choice in personal relationships?

8. Give an explanation of why patriarchy may be thought of as a structure with negative influences upon individuals.

9. Which sociologist studied the financial control that each partner in gay and lesbian couples had?

10. Which sociologist thought that the way sociologists investigate childhood is 'adultist'?

PRACTICE QUESTIONS

Item A

Our society has been defined by the power of the individual to make choices in constructing their own identity. This means they can pick and mix from many cultures, styles and eras to make themselves. Older ties that bound us to traditional fixed identities have disappeared. This choice applies to the families we create.

Many would agree that we have unprecedented choice but would argue that other, older or more traditional, influences still play a major part in making decisions about the families people live in.

Question 1 (AS and A Level style): Applying material from Item A and your knowledge, evaluate the postmodern view of the family. (20 marks) **Spend 30 minutes on your response.**

HINTS TO HELP YOU RESPOND

Do not be confused by the item or the question. The examiner may use the term postmodern to refer to family life views as this is one of the key areas of thought that create the personal life view. Show your knowledge of this connection when setting out your essay. You will be evaluating the family life view as the postmodern view. Make each point and illustrate with an example. Describing the view as giving a new tool to uncover some of the complex meanings that individuals give to relationships within families is a good start. Illustrate with some of the different meanings that people give to families today: fictive kin, importance of dead relatives (people are often named after a dead relative), pets as family and chosen families. All these points can be evaluated by the functionalist viewpoint. Most people are moving towards a nuclear family or have been in one so the functionalist emphasis on studying this family type has value. Spend some time explaining the contribution that has been made to our understanding of the relationships that gay and lesbian couples have because of the family life view that is derived from the postmodern view; likewise with the new sociology of childhood. Your conclusion will probably find that in an age of increasing family diversity the postmodern view is very important as it has given us new emphasis on the meanings that individuals themselves give to their relationships within families and what counts as family.

Question 2 (AS Level style): Define the term 'heteronormativity' (2 marks) **Spend no more than 3 minutes on your response.**

HINTS TO HELP YOU RESPOND

With a two mark question, your response must be short and precise. By defining a term, state what the term is without using any words from the term itself, e.g. 'The forces that exist to pressure a person into seemingly conforming to heterosexual patterns of behaviour.'

Demography

Demography is the term used to describe the study of human populations; that is, the characteristics, structure and changes to the population over time. Two factors lead to increased population – births and immigration. Two factors lead to decreased population — deaths and emigration. To find out the **net migration** of a country subtract the number of emigrants from the number of immigrants. To calculate the **natural change** in population subtract the number of deaths from births. The UK's population should reach 71 million by 2031, growing from 38 in 1901 to 65 million today. Before 1980 the increase was caused by natural change; since then, the increase has been caused by net migration. 'In the UK, the percentage of live births to women born outside the UK rose to 26·3% in 2015, compared with 25·7% in 2014' (Office for National Statistics). This is because women born outside the UK have higher fertility and are often working age adults.

The causes of migration are: **push factors** – persecution (religious or political), famine, war, unemployment and poverty – which cause people to leave their own country. Also **pull factors** – education, study, career, jobs, relatives and higher standards of living – attract people to a particular country.

Migration has caused a recent **baby boom** (an increase in the **birth rate**) as families from Eastern Europe usually have larger families. (There were baby booms following both world wars and in the 1960s.) Eastern Europeans are more religious and so view contraception differently and perhaps put family before individualism.

The **birth rate** is the number of live births per thousand of the population each year. The **total fertility rate** is the average number of children women will have during their child-bearing years (15–44). Because women are delaying having their first child to, on average, the age of 30, the fertility rate is declining. Both birth rate and total fertility rate have been falling in the UK since 1900. The **death rate** (the number of deaths per thousand of the population per year) has fallen, linked to increased **life expectancy** (an estimate of how long a person is expected to live). The **infant mortality rate** (IMR), the number of deaths of babies in their first year of life per one thousand live births of the population per year, has fallen. There are a number of linked factors explaining the decline in birth rate, death rate and infant mortality rate and increased life expectancy.

EVALUATION POINT

When analysing migrant influence it is important to note that only 5% of migrants are **asylum seekers** (escaping persecution, war, torture); most migrants to the UK are here to work or to study. There has been a history of negative attitudes towards poor non-white migrants to the UK and this continues with the negative attitudes to asylum seekers who are labelled as 'scroungers' and treated as dehumanised prisoners. Growing world interconnectedness has made it easier for migration to happen – this is called **globalisation**. **Undocumented workers** do not have permission to work in the UK. Estimates of 500 000 to 800 000 have been made; they are smuggled in by people-traffickers and are open to abuse and exploitation. Migration causes greater **cultural diversity** as people from different cultures meet. **EU migrants** made up more than a third of migrants to the UK.

EVALUATION POINT

McKeown identified environmental factors as being key to the decline in the death rate (from 18 in 1000 in 1902 to 9 in 1000 in 2012) and the increased life expectancy: e.g. public hygiene and sanitation improvements, better diet and nutrition, improved living standards. These have had more impact than medical advancements: e.g. inoculations against polio, typhoid, diphtheria. A key factor is that with more babies surviving, women choose to have fewer babies. This is important in the so-called 'March of Progress' for women in society.

Public health and welfare have been critical in influencing birth rates, death rates, life expectancy and the IMR (which has fallen from 134 in 1902 to 4·1 in 2012). Better housing with clean, safe drinking water and a wider range of food being available are the most fundamental changes. Advances in surgery and the development of antibiotics and penicillin have also contributed to the increased life expectancy.

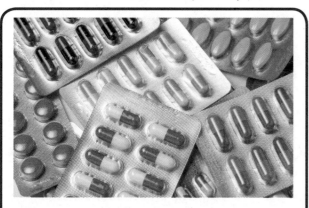

Advances in medicine has led to the development of antibiotics, which has resulted in an increased life expectancy.

EVALUATION POINT

When asked to explain the change in birth rate or total fertility rate it is vital to consider the changing attitudes of women, as examined in other topics. Women delay childbirth for careers and extend their education rather than start families. Career paths are open to women because of the gains made by feminists in shaping modern society. Many women will remain childless as their career success becomes of primary importance, not motherhood. Ease of divorce and access to abortion and contraception are reasons for the decline in birth rate. Children are no longer seen as an economic asset but an economic liability – that is, they require a huge financial investment from parents. In the past children worked and contributed to the household economy. Now, however, in our child-centred society, children expect to have high standards of living and this means families are now smaller.

Dependency ratio – the relationship between those working and those not working (dependent) – has become a key concern. In 1900 life expectancy for men and women was 50 and 57. Improved conditions of work, less dangerous occupations (from mining to service industries), the development of a welfare state (NHS), action on environmental pollution, all contribute to the rise in life expectancy and consequent increase in the dependency ratio. While fewer children have reduced the dependency ratio there are worries about the UK having an ageing population. This increases the amount of money spent on healthcare, as pensioners have more healthcare concerns. Vital skills are lost when people retire. If the elderly are infirm they may have to be cared for by relatives; that results in stress on the family. Ageing individuals continuing to live in their family homes may intensify a housing shortage.

EVALUATION POINT

There are many advantages to an ageing population, e.g. with the extension of the retirement age experienced and skilled employees are retained in the workforce, the fit older population contribute to society through taxes. The impact of the **grey pound** (the spending power of older people) boosts the economy as they spend on goods and services. Through voluntary work they contribute to society in a broader role (58% of over 65s volunteer). The elderly offer support to the rest of the family, financially and through childcare (looking after the grandchildren). There is also less crime because the elderly are more likely to obey the rules of society. Older people should not be stereotyped or given stigmatised identities.

The Griffith Report (1983) tried to develop a strategy for coping with long-term care of the elderly and mentally ill by outlining a plan for care in the community.

SUMMARY

- Demography is the study of population.
- The population of the UK has grown through natural change and net migration.
- Globalisation has had a major impact on migration.
- Push and pull factors are responsible for migration patterns.
- A recent baby boom is due to migration.
- A set of interrelated factors is responsible for declining birth rates, death rates and infant mortality rates.
- The changed position of women in society is one of these factors.
- Contraception, abortion and societal attitudes – easier divorce – are important for understanding the falling birth rate.
- Factors influencing the fall in death rate include: better housing, sanitation, public health developments, hygiene developments, medical knowledge and skills.
- The dependency ratio is a concern that affects social policy decisions on how to cope with the implications of an ageing population.

QUICK TEST

1. Why is it that babies of women from outside the UK made up more than a quarter of the births registered in the UK in 2015?

2. Give two examples of push factors affecting migration.

3. Give two examples of pull factors affecting migration.

4. How many baby booms has the UK experienced since 1900?

5. Define the 'infant mortality rate'.

6. Define the 'total fertility rate'.

7. What is meant by the term 'economic liability'?

8. Why might an ageing population be a cause for concern for governments?

9. Why might an increased life expectancy intensify a housing shortage?

10. One advantage of an ageing population is the impact of the 'grey pound'. Explain what this means.

PRACTICE QUESTIONS

Item A

A falling birth rate has led to some sociologists believing that some children will experience lonelier childhoods. The positive side of this is that the dependency ratio is brought down. Also the number of schools would be reduced. Some see this as an opportunity to invest in an increasing population of old people. They often require more care and increase the dependency ratio.

However there are concerns that old people are being stereotyped as dependent and useless.

Question 1 (AS and A Level style): Applying material from Item A and your knowledge, evaluate the view that an ageing population creates problems for society. (20 marks) **Spend 30 minutes on your response.**

HINTS TO HELP YOU RESPOND

You can see that the item gives you some positive and negative impacts of an ageing population to begin your essay with. It is important that you show a clear understanding of the concept of 'dependency', so explain this clearly from the outset. The next step is to set out the 'problems' or negatives clearly. The problems are often socially constructed (see pages 80–81) or, according to Marxists, structural, in that the old are seen as past their usefulness to capitalism (see pages 88–89). The other problems affect social policy decisions so make sure you evaluate these negatives by arguing how they present us with a chance to make policy shifts that benefit generations to come, such as the creation of the welfare state. Each problem can be countered with a positive impact. For example: 'People living longer means they remain in their homes for longer; however, they can be offered incentives to move if housing was built that catered for their needs. The benefits are also that we are more active and living healthier lives now and can contribute to the economy for longer.'

Question 2 (AS Level style): Using one example briefly explain how migration may affect the total fertility rate. (2 marks) **Spend 3 minutes on your response.**

HINTS TO HELP YOU RESPOND

A clearly explained example is all you need here; that means a one-sentence response. You may know more but you must save your time for longer essay style answers. Your answer may be: 'Migrants are usually working-age adults and so the total fertility rate may increase as those coming to a country are of child-bearing age.'

Families: Changes in the Family Over Time

Divorce was costly and difficult to obtain before the 20th century. Couples would separate but were still bound by law and religious obligations to one another. Society took seriously vows made before God, and these attitudes prevented diversity of families. Attitudes have changed, as society has become more **secular** (less religious) and divorce less **stigmatised** (carrying social disapproval/a negative label). Functionalists such as Ronald Fletcher believe that divorce rates are higher because there are rising expectations of marriage. People marry now for love and are not bound together by economic necessity. It is the **ideology of love** that leads to unrealistic expectations of marriage or relationships gleaned from the media; once love withers, the marriage dies.

The divorce process used to be costly and difficult before the 20th century.

The ideology of love does fit the increasing move towards individualisation and the pursuit of personal happiness. Women, through the work of feminist movements, have gained much greater freedom to reject unhappy marriages of exploitation and/or abuse.

EVALUATION POINT

The legal changes are key here. The Matrimonial Causes Act 1923 provided women with the same grounds for divorce as men. The Legal Aid and Advice Act 1949 allowed poor people help in getting a divorce, as the process was costly. In 1969 the Divorce Reform Act was passed, which meant that one, both or either of the partners did not have to be in the wrong (adultery, for example) to allow for divorce – they just needed to prove 'irretrievable breakdown of the marriage'. A two-year separation was enough for divorce or five years if one partner fought the divorce. The New Right would view rising divorce rates as having a destructive impact on society with people being allowed to 'give up' on marriage too easily. Feminists would argue that divorce allows women to flee from patriarchal oppression or male-dominated family life and to not have to live in 'empty-shell marriages' without love or commitment.

Women Have Greater Equality

Women have gained a much more equal footing within society. They have access to benefits to support them and their children without a male breadwinner but, more importantly, have equal opportunities in education and in the labour market. More than two-thirds of divorce petitions come from women. (Remember the work on pages 76–77 and the growing symmetry of relationships.) Sexual morality has been lessened because the church has less influence. Contraception is widely available and free from the NHS. Financial independence allows for self-interest or individualism to take even stronger hold in society. The young move away from parental supervision and make choices about marriage, cohabitation or same-sex relationships. That choice involves delaying marriage and extending cohabitation.

Although 42% of all marriages end in divorce, marriage itself is still popular. Remarriage is increasing which leads to **serial monogamy** – marriage, divorce then remarriage. The general trend of both divorces and fewer marriages can be linked to increasing privatisation of the nuclear family; this shields the couple from supportive influences or pressures that may keep the pair together in times of crisis. There are no places of refuge for either person as they try to overcome problems. Expectations of each partner on the marriage have increased as the other functions of the family have been reduced; this accompanies the increase in life expectancy and adds to the importance of love and companionship as reasons to be married over economic necessity.

The same points of explanation can be roughly used to understand the later age of marriage or the rise of singletons and the rise in cohabitation (unmarried couples living together), as well as the rise of **Living Apart Together** couples (LATs). The British Social Attitudes Survey in 2013 found that many couples were not financially ready to cohabit or marry, or were happier maintaining financial independence because of problems with previous partners. Couples that live apart but class themselves as in a long-term committed relationship comprise 10% of the adult population. Cohabiting couples are increasing; the figure was 2·9 million in 2013. Some couples regard cohabitation as a 'trial marriage'.

EVALUATION POINT

Although cohabiting is increasing, Robert Chester regarded this as a sign of the rise of the **neo-conventional family** ('neo' meaning new); it is not a threat to the stability and traditions provided by marriage and nuclear families. People cohabiting can arrive from previous monogamous marriages and be on their way to becoming married and forming conventional nuclear families. The couples are dual-earner income households or symmetrical.

Other Forms of Diversity of Family Type

There are growing numbers of lone-parent families; women's financial independence, greater individual choice, feminist ideas, rising divorce rates and changing attitudes have led to an increase in lone-parent families. A quarter of all families can be classed as lone-parent families. **Reconstituted families** or step-families make up more than one in ten of families with dependent children. Some sociologists see children within these families being at greater risk of poverty while others see the tensions and problems as similar to those in 'intact' families. Same-sex marriage and civil partnerships have increased because of greater acceptance within society; the law now allows for both of these as a legal option. Some regard this as a normalisation of the homosexual community. There are also ethnic differences in family types. 13% of the United Kingdom are ethnically diverse or not white British. Within the black community there are higher numbers of lone-parent female-headed households. Explanations for this are that poverty affects this community and creates unemployment that pushes men out of the family. Women have been presented as more independent, a legacy of slavery when families were forcibly split and women had to cope on their own. The picture is reversed in the Asian community where very few lone-parent families are found in comparison to black or white lone-parent families. Asian families have slightly higher numbers of children but most are nuclear in structure.

EVALUATION POINT

With the ageing population single-person households will become more significant. There is also a trend towards remaining single with the age of first marriage being 30 for women. Divorce creates single-person households, mainly men as the children remain with mothers.

SUMMARY

- Diversity of families is a result of declining stigma towards divorce, singlehood, same-sex relationships.

- The secularisation of society goes hand in hand with the decline of stigma.

- Divorce has increased owing to changes in law, the rise of individualism, the changed functions of the family, the rise of feminism and the changed position of women in society more generally.

- The ideology of love creates a need to feel totally fulfilled within marriage, emotionally and through the true love of total companionship.

- The Divorce Reform Act (1969) has had a significant impact leading to serial monogamy.

- Increased life expectancy has put greater strain on marriages.

- Reconstituted or step-families are found widely throughout society.

- Ethnicity does play a part in influencing family structures, through cultural legacies.

QUICK TEST

1. Why did Ronald Fletcher believe that divorce rates are high?

2. Which gender makes the most petitions for divorce?

3. Which theoretical perspective views easier access to divorce as harmful to society?

4. Which key term is used to describe a series of monogamous marriages a person may have within a lifetime?

5. What does the acronym LAT mean?

6. What is the term given to the process by which the influence of the church is declining?

7. What is social stigma?

8. What was the number of cohabiting couples in 2013?

9. Give three reasons why women have greater equality in contemporary society.

10. Give the defining characteristic of what Robert Chester called the 'neo-conventional' family.

PRACTICE QUESTIONS

Item A

Smaller family sizes and increased life expectancy have led to what Julia Brannen called **beanpole families**; these are families with few siblings but in which the family tree is extended to three generations – like a beanpole the families are long and thin. Anthony Giddens has argued that people may divorce more often because they seek the 'pure relationship' based on each partner's own personal fulfilment within the relationship.

Question 1 (A Level style): Applying material from Item A, analyse two changes to society that have led to greater diversity of families. (10 marks) **Spend 15 minutes on your response.**

HINTS TO HELP YOU RESPOND

In this response you are asked to 'analyse'. This means separate information into components and identify their characteristics or, put more simply, identify the underlying causes of increased diversity of family forms. The item does contain two examples of changes: individualisation and changing life expectancy. To reach the highest level of marks you must provide some evaluation of the impact of these points and link to the sociological web of ideas each of these points relates to. For example, increased personal freedoms and choices depend on greater wealth, the reduced influence of gender-role normalisation linked to greater gender equality. The higher levels of evaluation can be done by voicing the disapproval of the New Right at the undermining of traditional nuclear families. Develop this further by suggesting that the neo-conventional family is little different from the traditional nuclear family. This would be one paragraph, then write about, for example, the decline of the stigma attached to lone-parent families or same-sex relationships.

Item B

Women can support a family without a man due to equal pay and anti-discrimination laws. A woman who feels exploited by an asymmetrical relationship where traditional norms of breadwinner and homemaker have been internalised by their partner can choose to divorce that person. Some sociologists argue that traditional norms of duty and social responsibility have been eroded by self-interest and so women are choosing to put themselves first.

Question 2 (AS and A Level style): Applying material from Item B and your knowledge, evaluate the view that the changed position of women within society is the greatest contributor to changed patterns of divorce since the 1970s. (20 marks) **Spend 30 minutes on your response.**

HINTS TO HELP YOU RESPOND

You must explain in detail the changed position of women, of course, but link this to other changes such as the rise of the 'new man', greater symmetry between couples, the rise of individualism more generally. Remember to link to theoretical viewpoints, that is, those that approve of the changed position of women (feminists) and those that disapprove (the New Right). You must also list the other factors and perhaps show how they are interrelated: secularisation, declining stigma, increased life expectancy, the ideology of love. From this view it is difficult to judge a single factor as they support each other in changing the divorce rate. The legal changes can also be explored. Make your conclusion support the main points of your essay.

Families: Family Diversity

The main focus of this topic addresses the dominance of the nuclear family compared to other family types. Diversity of family forms existed in the past. Desertion (abandoning the family) and death of a spouse caused single-parent families or step-families. In contemporary society we have greater diversity of family types reflecting the greater choice and cultural diversity of society. Rhona and Robert Rapoport identified five types of diversity. Cultural diversity affects patterns of extended families, for example, based on ethnicity, culture and religion. Life-stage diversity affects your family type based on the stage of your life you are at: for example, a widowed pensioner may be a lone-person householder. Organisational diversity refers to the choices we can now make about how we organise our roles within families. Generational diversity refers to the moral and social attitudes towards relationships imparted by specific generational experiences, for example, more traditional segregated roles may be present among older couples. Social class diversity occurs because the money they earn and their class background give people different opportunities and attitudes to relationships and family life, for example, the dual burden would potentially fall more heavily on the shoulders of working class women, as they cannot afford to hire domestic help, in comparison to more affluent middle class women.

The Individualisation Thesis

Both Anthony Giddens (1992) and Ulrich Beck (1992) advanced this theory. The old ties that influenced our choices have been replaced by individual decisions and choices about relationships. In the past a person's social class or their gender or ethnicity was seen as fixed, whereas now individual choice dominates. For Giddens the **pure relationship** has replaced the normative controls of tradition and law. Couples negotiate relationships based on equality and individual choice. Each person prioritises their own needs within the relationship. Love, sex and personal happiness have replaced duty, tradition and obligation. This has led to increased uncertainty and instability and consequently greater diversity as an individual chooses what is best for him- or herself.

EVALUATION POINT

Beck agreed with Giddens that greater gender equality and individualism are features of contemporary families. He argued that this has led to the **negotiated family** where members agree what is best for themselves by agreement. Again, Beck suggested that these families are less stable leading to **zombie families**. The members seek stability in families but they are inherently unstable as there are no traditions or laws to bind the unit; just as a zombie appears to be living but is actually dead, so it is with the modern family. The personal life perspective challenges the extent of personal choice. Smart and May suggested that people cannot make free choices as they all have a social context where norms operate to influence choice. Patriarchal values are still powerful influences as are social class and economic factors. Research focuses on the white middle classes and skews our view of individual choice and freedom.

EVALUATION POINT

The New Right are resistant to family diversity. Both Benson and Morgan cited evidence that monogamous marriage is the most stable environment in which to raise children. Men and women benefit from the increased motivation of men within these relationships to provide for their family. Men are less likely to be unemployed, are more likely to earn higher wages, and couples with children who are married are less likely to separate than cohabiting couples. Murphy's study of ONS data on cohabiting couples supported this negative view, showing children of cohabiting couples do worse in education and are more prone to illness.

Connectedness Thesis

Carol Smart (2011) has argued that the decisions we make are all made in a context of a complex network of relationships, e.g. the impact on relatives and friends. No individual makes a decision without considering this network of connected interests. Finch and Mason (1993) supported this idea with their research into extended families and the obligations that still exist to other family members when an individual makes decisions. Individuals cannot break from their past relationships with which they have become interwoven without considering the interests of others.

EVALUATION POINT

The New Right, supported by many conservative politicians, regard any family that is not a 'cereal packet' family as broken. From this perspective personal choices undermine stability in society and allow for the shirking of commitment, both personally and to the wider stability of society. The New Right argue that the conventional heterosexual monogamous nuclear family has been undermined by modern or progressive laws; the ease of divorce is a prime example of this for the New Right. Feminist writers regard these views as deliberately trying to prevent equality and the advancement of women's rights. Critics of the New Right also suggest that the New Right ignore the economic factors that cause relationships to fail.

Postmodern Views

Postmodern ideas suggest that we live in a world that is at a very different stage to other stages of history. ('Post' means after.) We have reached a stage in history 'after' the modern era of industrialised modern societies. This stage in history is characterised by unprecedented personal choices. We can create our own identities by picking and mixing styles from many eras. Social changes happen rapidly and, combined with the unprecedented choice, allows for greater diversity of family structures. Like Beck and Giddens, postmodern writers highlight the instability that choice brings with it. Stacey (1998) saw choices giving greater freedom to women to actively decide on how to structure their relationships at any particular moment in their lives. Morgan (1997) supported this notion of active personal agency and argued this means it is impossible to make generalisations about the developments of family structures, as a family is whatever people themselves decide it is. Life course analysis supports this postmodern analysis using unstructured interviews to examine the meanings that people themselves give to family structures.

EVALUATION POINT

There are points in common between many of the theorists above and it is important to note that postmodern ideas have influenced many sociological studies even when those studies were reacting against some of the ideas of postmodern theory. Central to the changes is the changed position of women in society, delaying families for careers and having fewer children (cost and lower total fertility rate). All these factors are covered in various topics throughout the book and should be drawn on in your evaluations.

Women nowadays often delay having a family in favour of pursuing their career.

SUMMARY

- There was diversity of family types in the past but not to the extent found today.

- Rapoport and Rapoport have found diversity of family types takes five forms: cultural, life-stage, organisational, generational and social class.

- The New Right argue that diversity of family types is bad for the individual members of families and for society more generally.

- The individualisation thesis allows for greater personal choice in creating family relationships.

- The pure relationship is based on the individual needs of each person.

- The negotiated family represents individuals doing what is best for him/herself by reasoned negotiation with others in the family.

- People are not free to make choices about relationships, as structures still exist that affect 'free choice' and a context of connected relationships act as a force on those decisions.

- The postmodern age we live in is based on the unprecedented choices we now can make as individuals. This has benefited women.

QUICK TEST

1. Rapoport and Rapoport identify culture and social class as types of family diversity. What are the three other types of diversity?

2. What is the New Right view of family diversity?

3. Which sociologist suggested that couples now have 'pure relationships'?

4. Which two factors are pure relationships based on?

5. Which theorist suggested that negotiated families have led to zombie families?

6. Which sociologist argued in the connectedness thesis that individuals make decisions within a complex network of interrelated factors?

7. Sociologists Smart and May argued that we are not entirely free to choose relationships because of other factors. State two of these factors.

8. Give three defining features of the postmodern age.

9. Identify the research method used to uncover the meanings people give their lives by sociologists who use 'life course' analysis.

10. Identify the negative consequence that sociologists agree is brought about by greater personal choice in relationships.

PRACTICE QUESTIONS

Item A
Matrifocal families are families that have a female head, and some commentators have seen the increased numbers of these households as bringing instability. Others, such as Chester, argue that the traditional nuclear family continues to be the most popular choice for couples with cohabitation a step on the path to conventional family forms. 12·3 million families out of a total of 18·2 million were a married couple in the UK in 2013. Chester recognised that dual-income households are the new norm or neo-conventional family. Diversity and choice in relationships has been perhaps overstated and should not be regarded as a threat to societal stability.

Question 1 (A Level style): Applying material from Item A and your knowledge, analyse two changes to society that threaten the stability of the traditional nuclear family. (10 marks) **Spend 15 minutes on your response.**

HINTS TO HELP YOU RESPOND
In this response you are asked to 'analyse'. This means separate information into components and identify their characteristics or, put more simply, identify the underlying reasons why people choose to live outside the traditional nuclear family. The item does contain a huge clue as to what to write on, such as 'choice' and 'diversity'. To reach the highest level of marks you must provide some evaluation of the impact of these points and link to the sociological web of ideas each of these points relates to. For example, some like the New Right see the impact of greater equality as detrimental to traditional roles; this is disputed by feminist thinkers so you must state why feminists disagree.

Item B
Families of choice are the kin and friends selected by same-sex couples to make up a supportive network and are often cited as an example of the level of choice available to individuals in creating their 'families' beyond the narrower confines of the traditional nuclear family. For some, the law has followed the broader social changes and reinforced personal choice. For others, the law has facilitated the erosion of traditional family types. Easier divorce and state benefits that allow the existence of increased numbers of lone-parent families lead to ill-disciplined children, delinquency and educational failure of children. This means poor families remain poor and a burden to the state.

Question 2 (AS and A Level style): Applying material from Item B and your knowledge, evaluate the view that the growth of family diversity has led to the decline of the traditional nuclear family. (20 marks) **Spend 30 minutes on your response.**

HINTS TO HELP YOU RESPOND
There are many ways to reach a conclusion on the topic and many differing conclusions you can arrive at. If you look back at the two previous topics you see the amount of material that is useful in answering this question. It is probably easiest to put forward the New Right view that supports the point made in the question and stated in the item. Use specific arguments and draw on pages 84–85 and 112–113 for more detail. Use feminist or conflict theories to dispute the extent of changes and show the postmodern views as a way of evaluating both New Right and feminist views. Always link your paragraphs to a direct response to the question and evidence the points you make. Emphasise that the nuclear family form is dominant; cite Robert Chester here. Summarise the trends towards greater choice and the consequent instability of relationships.

Social Policy and the Family

Social policies are the actions taken by governments to improve social situations: protect children from exploitation, improve housing for the population, tackle unemployment or provide solutions for an ageing population. These policies are put into action through changes in laws and through acts of parliament. Policies have a huge impact on education and families. Different political parties have different views on how to improve conditions for families. This is because they have different worldviews or **ideologies**.

Social policies, like improving housing for the population, are set by the government to try to improve social situations.

The New Right has a **familial ideology**; this means it has a specific and narrow definition of what a family should be – with roles that are traditional and gendered, with children respecting adult authority completely. They view family diversity as damaging to social stability. The heterosexual traditional nuclear family is seen as fundamental to a healthy, stable and safe society. The New Right view is a political view. This viewpoint has been very influential on government policies and is based on the writings of **Charles Murray**. Murray argued that over-generous welfare benefits encouraged diverse family types, single-parent, female-headed households that were responsible for raising a generation of children that formed an **underclass** dependent on welfare benefits. These benefits did nothing to encourage fathers to remain as role models for their children. Boys would grow up without stable male role models within a **dependency culture**, content to remain on over-generous welfare benefits and a burden to the state. Further, benefits were a **perverse incentive** to not seek gainful employment, as the benefits encouraged behaviour against the interests of wider society and the individuals themselves, who would remain disruptive, prone to lawlessness and part of the underclass.

EVALUATION POINT

The welfare state was created after the Second World War to fight the five social evils: poverty, idleness, disease, squalor and ignorance. They formed the basis of the NHS and better social housing. Later, the feminist movements established hard fought parity through the Equal Pay Act (1970) and the Sex Discrimination Act (1975). Then in the 21st century gay relationships were recognised through civil partnerships and then gay marriage. It seems that the New Right think these changes should be reversed as they oppose gay marriage and seek a return to traditional gendered heterosexual roles for men and women.

The policies of the New Right are apparent in government legislation from Conservative to New Labour to the Coalition government and through to the present Conservative government.

Government	Policy supporting New Right views	Policy supporting New Right views	Policy against New Right views
Conservatives – Thatcher/ Major years (1979–1997)	Local authorities were banned from promoting homosexuality.	Child Support Agency to track down absent fathers and make them pay to support their children.	Ease of access to divorce.
New Labour – Blair/Brown years (1997–2010)	Parenting Orders gave parents sharp reminders of their responsibilities to stop truancy/offending.	The heterosexual family was preferred over other types.	Tolerance and support of dual-income earner households and single-parent households through maternity leave, Family Tax Credits to support poorer working families
Coalition government – Cameron/Clegg (2010–2015)	Troubled Families Policy (2012) – to tackle the damage and strain that families from the 'underclass' cause; irresponsible parenting by dad-less divorcees. David Cameron blamed 'broken families' for the London riots of 2011.	Austerity – cuts to welfare: benefits, NHS, education and other public services that poorer families (and the middle classes) rely on.	Gay marriage introduced, adoption laws equalised for gay couples

EVALUATION POINT

Feminist sociologist Diana Leonard (1978) viewed social policies as reinforcing **patriarchal ideology** and not supporting equality. Policies assume men play the instrumental or breadwinner role. Giving women more maternity leave than men reinforces subordinate gender-role socialisation and socially constructs men as the breadwinner and women as mother, carer and nurturer.

Jacques Donzelot (1977) viewed social policy from a conflict perspective and is critical of social policies as they seek to monitor and surveil. This means that the systems of welfare, social care and expertise are in place to **police families**. Experts such as social workers use their knowledge to position themselves as the professionals exercising power over, and so control, the behaviours of poorer or working class families. This idea of power being diffused through the relationships within society is applied from the work of Michel Foucault who examined how liberal democracies kept control over their citizens. Donzelot specifically identified the poor as a group within society that are monitored and controlled by this system of policing by expertise. Knowledge is power in this analysis and exerts pressure on poorer families to conform to social norms through, for example, court judgements such as compulsory parenting orders (whereby the parents go to classes to learn how to parent responsibly).

EVALUATION POINT

Functionalists would completely disagree with this view of social policy. The laws enacted by governments support the **value consensus**. Beyond this social policies have begun to tackle the so-called 'five social evils'. This is evidenced by the **March of Progress**. We have better healthcare systems and welfare provisions (pensions, child protection laws, every child matters legislation to safeguard children from exploitation and neglect).

SUMMARY

- Social policies are the actions that governments take to improve society, e.g. laws affecting families, housing or education.
- The New Right has been a big influence on family policies.
- The familial ideology of the New Right promotes the heterosexual traditional nuclear family with distinct gendered roles for men and women.
- Charles Murray believed that social policies (the welfare state) had damaged society by creating an underclass.
- The New Right believe that lone-parent families were encouraged by state benefits that encouraged a dependency culture.
- Feminists believe that social policies reinforce patriarchal ideologies.
- Donzelot argued that state policies police families by empowering experts such as doctors to carry out surveillance on poor families so they are controlled.
- Functionalists view state policies as beneficial to all members of society.

QUICK TEST

1. What are social policies?

2. What is meant by the 'familial ideology'?

3. Who is the main influence behind the formulation of 'New Right' thinking?

4. Which key term describes the idea that generous welfare benefits encourage families to continue to live off benefits?

5. What are poverty, squalor, ignorance, disease and idleness known as?

6. What was the name of the agency that was introduced to try to force absent fathers to face their responsibilities and provide financially for their children?

7. The Coalition government introduced a policy to combat dad-less and so called 'broken families' that were seen as the cause of the London riots. What was the policy called?

8. Which sociologist saw social policies as reinforcing patriarchal ideologies?

9. What is the aim of social policy according to Jacques Donzelot?

10. What evidence do functionalists have that social policies support the value consenus (shared norms and values that benefit individuals and society at large)?

PRACTICE QUESTIONS

Item A

Tax and benefits are thought to prioritise men as playing the instrumental role. This and childcare legislation continue to enforce the patriarchal ideology according to feminists. Some feminists would disagree, arguing that great strides have been made to promote greater equality in society through social policies.

Question 1 (A Level style): Applying material from Item A, analyse two views of the effects of social policy on the family. (10 marks) **Spend 15 minutes on your response.**

HINTS TO HELP YOU RESPOND

Here you must discuss two effects that are mentioned in the item. Be careful to pick them out before you start your response. You will see that the patriarchal family structure is one effect (you could mention Charles Murray and the familial ideology). Be sure to write in depth; you should explain any concepts, theorists or theories that you use in your response and add an analysis of the views you identify (a contrasting point). Do not include an introduction; spend 5 minutes on each effect. For example: 'The male breadwinner role is part of the patriarchal ideology that seeks to keep women dominated, controlled and subordinate to men. Traditional nuclear family structures are often favoured by legislation which seeks to punish other family types as inferior or deviant.' Evaluate by arguing that Charles Murray has found that social policies have created a dependency culture among an underclass of single-parent, female-headed families. The greater the level of detail in your response (ensured by the PEEL structure of point, evidence, explain and link back to the question) the smarter your answer.

Question 2 (AS Level style): Outline three ways in which social policies can affect family structures. (6 marks) **Spend 9 minutes on your response.**

HINTS TO HELP YOU RESPOND

Your response here will be quite short. For each 'way' start a new line to show the examiner that you are outlining another point. You could discuss a range of theoretical views on social policies and how they impact on families. From a New Right position social policies can encourage single-parent, dad-less families. Similarly, feminists insist that social policies encourage the heterosexual traditional nuclear family. Social policy can encourage greater family diversity through enabling women to sever relationships with abusive partners or have families on their own as single parents. Policies can also allow same-sex couples to adopt, thus creating more diversity of family structures. It is important that in each response you explain the impact on diversity or a restriction of family structures.

Model Answers and Quick Test Answers

Top Mark Question and Answers

Question 1 (AS Level style): Define the term 'formula funding'. (2 marks)

Top Mark Response:
Formula funding describes schools receiving an amount of money for each student who attends. Schools aim to attract more pupils to receive more funding.

> Here the respondent has explained what formula funding is and then simply given a brief example of how it works to ensure that they have fully defined it.

Question 2 (AS and A Level style): Outline three reasons why working class pupils are likely to underperform in the education system. (6 marks)

Top Mark Response:
- Working class pupils are likely to use a restricted language code. Teachers and textbooks use an elaborate language code; as a result working class pupils find it difficult to understand content covered in class.
- Working class pupils come from households that have low levels of income and as a result they may be materially deprived. This means that they may not have the physical necessities needed to perform well in school.
- Teachers are likely to label working class students negatively. They are likely to see them as removed from their view of the 'ideal pupil' and as a result working class pupils may develop a self-fulfilling prophecy and end up failing in the education system.

> The response takes the form of three short bullet points. The respondent has mentioned three reasons with a really brief explanation as to why each causes working class pupils to underperform. Each point is started on a new line.

Question 3 (A Level style): Outline and explain two roles that Marxists see the education system performing. (10 marks)

Top Mark Response:
Marxists state that the education system creates an obedient workforce. Bowles and Gintis noted that the education system does this in order to support the capitalist system. This system requires a proletariat workforce that is willing to wage-slave obediently in order to create wealth for the bourgeoisie. In a study of 237 New York high schools Bowles and Gintis found that the majority of schools rewarded obedient behaviour traits over those of independence or creativity. By creating a non-questioning obedient workforce the education system serves capitalist society which needs the labour of the proletariat.

Another role that Marxists suggest the education system serves is that of acting as an 'ideological state apparatus'. Louis Althusser believed that the education system establishes a level of control over the ideas, beliefs and values of the proletariat. In controlling the ideas of the proletariat the education system ensures that class inequality is reproduced from one generation to the next. It also legitimises class inequality, making the proletariat accept that their place in society is inevitable and that they must work hard in order to progress. This is called the 'myth of meritocracy', a belief that hard work will be rewarded; however, according to Marxists, the only group receiving rewards are the bourgeoisie.

> In this response two key roles are selected, that of obedience and also the concept of an ideological state apparatus. Each point is started in a new detailed paragraph. The roles are evidenced with sociologists and key terms to ensure a thorough explanation.

Question 4 (AS Level style): Evaluate the problems of using participant observation in sociological research. (16 marks)

Top Mark Response:
Interpretivist sociologists favour the use of participant observation as it gathers a wealth of qualitative data which, through its depth, is naturally valid. Sociologists are able to immerse themselves in the activity and group that they are observing. Through this awareness they can develop a real sense of insight and empathetic understanding of the group which they are observing.

It is, however, difficult to gain access to groups in order to conduct participant observation. Within any group dynamics there will be a number of gatekeepers whose permission must be sought in order to begin research. Groups will be wary of outsiders joining and may reject the sociologist planning to participate. There may also be difficulties when participating in certain activities, especially those which involve criminal activity. There are many practical problems presented in participant observation.

Sociologists may favour covert participant observation as it allows the researcher's identity and true research cause to remain hidden from those being researched. As a result of this, people being observed are not able to opt out of the study. This does, however, pose ethical issues. Sociologists are essentially deceiving participants by lying to them about their own identity within the group. This can cause trust issues within those being researched and is potentially ethically unsound. Covert research is, at times, unlikely to be approved by official bodies governing the research.

In order to resolve the issues of covert research sociologists may decide to make their participant observation overt, with their identity and research purpose known to those being studied. This can be devastating to results as participants are highly likely to experience the Hawthorne effect and change their behaviour as they are aware that they are being watched, causing issues with validity. When aware that a sociologist is observing, the level of authenticity is reduced for those being observed; although behaviour is likely to be affected ethical implications are clearly reduced. To counteract this change in behaviour sociologists may aim to become as much a part of the group as they can, striving to develop a strong rapport with those they are observing. By developing this rapport sociologists may struggle to remain objective; they will naturally empathise with the group and could potentially end up 'going native', becoming completely subjective and possibly glamourising the lifestyles of those they are observing. In critique of this the subjective involvement of the researcher may lead to verstehen and as a result gather a higher level of validity.

In order to participate in their observation the sociologist must remain a part of the group. It is difficult to obtain detailed findings from short periods of observation. As a result of this, participant observation is highly time consuming; by 'acting' as one of the group sociologists may have to be skilfully trained. They must also strive to stay in the group in order to examine them fully, maintaining a 'cover' for a long time can be difficult. This means that practical problems may impact on the sociologist.

Noting the findings of participant observation is a hard task to manage. The data gathered will be highly detailed and extremely hard to analyse. As the findings of participant observation are qualitative, positivist sociologists reject the method as it fails to discover representative and reliable patterns of cause and effect relationships. However, although these are problems, the method also produces rich and qualitative data as a result.

The rich validity of participant observation is clearly a true strength of the method. However, its ethical implications and lack of reliability and representativeness far outweigh these benefits. A sociologist may aim to use triangulation in order to achieve findings that use qualitative and quantitative methods.

> There is a conclusion here which ties the response back to the question asked.

Item A
Sociological research has identified that teachers label students based upon their own ideas of the 'ideal pupil'. Some students feel the impact of negative labels, others benefit from the teacher's positive judgement. Labels can be created by teachers according to a pupil's social class, ethnicity or gender. These labels can lead to a self-fulfilling prophecy.

Unstructured interviews have been favoured by many sociologists as a means of investigating the impact of labels applied by teachers on students. They have a range of benefits and pitfalls when used to study phenomena in education. The effectiveness of the unstructured interviews, when applied to education, is highly debated.

Question 5 (AS and A Level style): Applying material from Item A and your own knowledge of research methods, evaluate the strengths and limitations of unstructured interviews for studying the impact of the self-fulfilling prophecy on pupil achievement. (20 marks)

Top Mark Response:
Interpretivist sociologists prefer the use of unstructured interviews when researching the impact of the self-fulfilling prophecy on pupil achievement. They like that the method gathers richly detailed, valid findings which can be used to measure the meanings that people involved in education attach to their treatment of others. As Item A suggests teachers label students based on their perception of the 'ideal pupil'. Unstructured interviews allow a detailed insight into the views of pupils and teachers, the two main groups involved in the self-fulfilling prophecy.

> The response starts with the theoretical perspective that would favour the method. It also uses the item and states that it is doing so. This is a requirement of the question. In order to create an effective response you should examine the item for key hooks to discuss when creating your plan.

Unstructured interviews are much like a guided conversation and allow the sociologist to develop a rapport with the interviewee. When interviewing teachers this rapport can lead to confidence in the teacher to respond truthfully about their views of students and how close they fit the view of the 'ideal pupil'. The teacher's confidence in the interviewer will ensure that they feel able to trust the interviewer to talk honestly about how their view of the pupil may mean that they treat the pupil differently. This causes the findings to be more truthful and therefore more valid.

> The essay clearly links the nature of the research method (how it ensures truthfulness through rapport) and links this directly with the nature of the self-fulfilling prophecy (how it is sensitive and teachers will need to trust researchers to discuss it). A good method in context essay will always aim to make specific links like this one.

As unstructured interviews gather a wealth of qualitative data, they help uncover the feelings and emotions of pupils. The sociologist is able to ask sensitive questions in order to discover how pupils feel about teachers and how they are treated by them. Unstructured interviews allow the researcher to give pupils time to ask their own questions – differing levels of ability mean that groups of students often need to clarify the questions asked. Sociologists are able to delve deeper, using probing questions to find out exactly why pupils act in certain ways in response to certain teachers, discovering the true impact of a teacher on an individual pupil and how their actions may be the result of the teacher's view of them.

Again another clear link between an unstructured interview allowing flexibility and the need for this in discovering how a teacher's labelling of a pupil may cause their behaviour to change.

One issue with unstructured interviews in order to study the impact of the self-fulfilling prophecy is that certain groups who are likely to be heavily affected by a self-fulfilling prophecy may not be present in school to interview; however, interviews at home are much more difficult to organise and gain permission for. Pupils from an anti-school subculture are most likely to be labelled as far from the view of the 'ideal pupil'. They are also more likely to truant from school and as a result may not be present when the sociologist wishes to conduct an interview.

Unstructured interviews require a dialogue between the interviewee and interviewer. Sociological research has suggested that pupils who receive negative labels from teachers and therefore become a self-fulfilling prophecy are likely to be working class. Working class pupils may be labelled as a result of the restricted language code that they use. This language code might also cause the sociologist difficulty in understanding the pupil. They may struggle to understand how the pupil feels about their teacher's judgement of them. However, the unstructured interview will also allow points to be clarified and understood by both interviewer and interviewee.

The respondent makes another direct link between the research method and the nature of the self-fulfilling prophecy. They make use of their own knowledge of the self-fulfilling prophecy in linking it to working class pupils and also pupils from an anti-school subculture.

It is evident that there are many advantages and disadvantages in using unstructured interviews to study the impact of the self-fulfilling prophecy. It may be better if the sociologist used triangulation, combining the method with a quantitative method in order to improve the reliability and representativeness of the results.

In concluding, the response uses triangulation as an alternative. It also uses the wording of the question in order to keep a focus on the question asked.

Item B
Official statistics suggest that working class students are at a significant disadvantage in the education system. Sociological research suggests that the attainment gap between middle and working class students may be a result of factors within the education system itself. Factors include the way that working class pupils are treated by teachers and also the subcultures that working class students are likely to fall into, putting them at a disadvantage.

Others believe the gap in achievement between social classes is the consequence of life outside school. Factors in the home lives of working class pupils impact on their ability to do well. These include not having the equipment needed to learn effectively at home.

Question 6 (A Level style): Applying material from Item B and your knowledge, evaluate the view that social class differences in educational achievement are largely the result of home background factors outside school itself. (30 marks)

Top Mark Response:
As Item B states, working class students are at a significant disadvantage in the education system. Schools often measure a pupil's class by looking at whether or not they have been eligible for free school meals; working class pupils are naturally from homes with lower incomes and therefore end up receiving free school meals. In 2011, only 63% of students who received free school meals achieved 5 A*–C grades at GCSE, compared with 83% of all other pupils in England. This suggests that there is a real gap in educational achievement between middle class and working class pupils.

In Item B the treatment of pupils by teachers is discussed. Howard Becker believed that working class pupils are often labelled negatively by teachers. He conducted interviews with 60 Chicago high school teachers, finding that teachers labelled pupils based on how closely they fitted their view of the 'ideal pupil'. Working class pupils were less likely to be close to 'ideal' for a variety of reasons, from uniform standards through to language used. This suggests that social class differences are a result of systems within school as teacher interaction takes place in the school setting.

In critique of labelling being a factor inside school, it is often clear that a pupil's demeanour causing them to be labelled is developed through their lifestyle at home. Basil Bernstein found that working class pupils and middle class pupils used different forms of speech. He noted that working class pupils use a restricted language code which consisted of basic vocabulary, a lack of correct grammar and simple sentences. Middle class pupils use an elaborated speech code, which involves the use of a much wider vocabulary and more complex sentence structure. Teachers use elaborated speech code and therefore fail to relate to working class pupils; they may label working class pupils more readily as they believe that their speech code denotes their ability. This would suggest that a level of speech developed through life outside school can cause working class underachievement, meaning that differences are a result of factors outside school itself.

Speech codes can certainly cause a barrier to a pupil's learning. However, this may not be a direct result of the code that the pupil uses, but more specifically the education system's lack of ability to address this and ensure that all people of all classes can access the curriculum. This is a real and significant failure of the system itself and means that school factors are largely to blame for class differences in achievement.

The treatment of pupils within school can cause a self-fulfilling prophecy to occur. Teachers' negative labels of working class pupils can be internalised by the pupils themselves. Once the pupil sees themselves as the negative label applied by the teacher they start to naturally become the label itself. For example, a pupil who is labelled 'lazy' may end up having such low expectations of themselves that they become 'lazy'. This labelling and response to it are factors within school and cannot be ignored. Rosenthal and Jacobson studied the self-fulfilling prophecy in action by deceiving high school teachers into the view that they had created a test to identify pupils who were naturally gifted. They identified a group of students as 'spurters' to staff at the school, though the group was simply selected at random. Upon returning to the school a year later, Rosenthal and Jacobson found that this group had progressed significantly over their peers, evidencing the view that social class differences are the result of in-school factors and processes.

Even though many sociologists suggest school itself is to blame, others see the lifestyle of the working class and their shared attitudes and values as a cause for underachievement. These factors outside school include an attitude of fatalism that many working class pupils share. Research suggests that working class children carry a fatalistic attitude instilled in them at home. They see no power in their own actions to change their social position. This view from outside school hampers progress and impacts on educational achievement. Coupled with this, Barry Sugarman noted that working class pupils crave immediate gratification, the need for instant rewards. As a result working class pupils are not willing to wait and work through education for the reward of a highly paid career; they prefer to leave education as soon as possible and immediately start earning wages in jobs that require little or no academic qualifications. Yet again a factor from outside school itself.

Item B mentions the impact of not having access to equipment that aids learning at home as a cause of working class pupils' underachievement. This lack of the physical necessities for educational success is known as 'material deprivation'. Material deprivation is a factor that comes from outside school. With working class families having lower incomes they may struggle to provide access to computers, tablets or learning websites. Material deprivation may also mean that working class pupils live in more cramped conditions with little or no space to complete home learning tasks without disruptions from other family members. Working class pupils may also have a poor diet, impacting on their ability to concentrate in class and also on their attendance levels in school.

It is clear that each of these factors from outside school can impact on a pupil's relationship with the teacher. This means that it is impossible to rule out any of the factors as a main cause of an educational achievement gap between the social classes. Examining the disadvantages of the working class may provide some answers; however, it may be better to look at the advantages that middle class pupils have.

Bourdieu found that middle class pupils have a 'cultural capital' over the working class. They share norms, values and beliefs that put them at an advantage in the education system. Middle class pupils have a knowledge that is passed from one generation to the next. Their parents are more likely to be in professional roles and be able to share their expertise, encouraging them to perform well in school. This out of school factor may be a main cause of class differences in achievement; it may also influence school factors. As a result of marketisation schools compete for the 'best' pupils. With their professional backgrounds middle class parents are likely to be skilled choosers of schools, selecting high performing schools for their child to attend. Working class parents do not have this cultural capital and are often 'disconnected-local choosers' of schools, simply selecting the most convenient school for their child regardless of results. Here it is clear that factors inside school and outside school are impossible to separate.

In conclusion, working class lifestyles, norms and values impact heavily on how pupils operate within a school setting. It could be argued that these factors from outside school fuel the differences that occur within school achievement.

> The conclusion uses the wording of the question to ensure that the response has not lost focus. It offers a simple link between internal and external factors.

Question 7 (AS Level style): Define the term 'net migration'. (2 marks)

Top Mark Response:
Net migration is the difference between immigration and emigration and this will show if the population is increasing or decreasing.

> A clear definition of how net migration figures are arrived at. The candidate indicates how this figure is significant to the change in population size. There is no need to explain each of the other terms used or to give explanations of birth rate and death rates as contributing to population size.

Question 8 (AS Level style): Using one example, briefly explain how family diversity can be affected by migration. (2 marks)

Top Mark Response:
Families will have a greater number of children in each family as migrant mothers have higher total fertility rates; they often do not delay children for careers and have more children.

> One clear example is used only, with an explanation that is accurately explained. Other ideas could have been: reluctance to divorce because of religious beliefs, or the number of extended family forms may increase because of the cultural differences in the types of family structure migrants have.

Question 9 (AS Level style): Outline three reasons why children are thought to be victims of age patriarchy. (6 marks)

Top Mark Response:
- Adults control children financially, restricting their ability to earn money and controlling their actions through rewards of pocket money.
- The spaces that a child can access or move around in are strictly controlled by adults; some children are not allowed out of their gardens or houses to play.
- Children's time is monitored and adults have power over every moment of a child's life. Through meal times, bed times and at school their days are divided up neatly by the routines of school life.

> The response takes the form of three clear and precise bullet points. The respondent has mentioned three reasons with a really brief explanation as to why each point supports the idea that children are under the power, control and authority of adults.

Question 10 (AS and A Level style): Outline and explain two ways in which the changes to the position of women has influenced family structures. (10 marks)

Top Mark Response:
Couples have become much more symmetrical in their structure. Symmetrical couples can be identified by the greater equality between the sexes. Symmetrical couples are said to have joint-conjugal roles where both share in all aspects of domestic labour, they do an equal amount of the household tasks and both are wage earners. This has come about because of a March of Progress that involves women gaining greater equality in the workplace and in the amount of money they earn. Radical feminists disagree with this view as they point to the dual burden that women now have to carry. Not only are women earning a living in careers, but they must also keep up the responsibilities of looking after the home. Gershuny found that men did adapt over time to more housework, which represented a lagged adaptation. Women adapted more naturally to changes as they saw housework as natural.

Women are putting off marriage to be educated and pursue careers, which means that there is an increase in cohabiting couples or single-person households as women now have economic independence supported by the Equal Pay Act. Women have fewer children as they pursue a career and on average do not have their first child until

30 years of age. Some New Right commentators, such as Charles Murray, argue that women are going against their biologically determined roles and this will damage society as they can too easily leave their husbands as they are ensured the financial independence to support themselves and even a child. These dad-less families without role models for sons are sources of instability in society which needs to return to the traditional nuclear family.

In this response two impacts on family structure are clearly explained. Each point is started in a new detailed paragraph. The changes to family structures are evidenced with sociologists and key terms to ensure a thorough explanation.

Item A
Social policies may be seen to treat men and women equally; there has been progress according to liberal feminists. This progress includes paternity leave for men and an extension of the amount of maternity leave that women can obtain to care for their newborn baby. Care of the elderly is underfunded and women do much of this care.

Question 11 (A Level Style): Applying material from Item A analyse two ways in which social policies reinforce a patriarchal ideology.

Top Mark Response:
Social policies do not treat men and women equally. Diana Leonard, a radical feminist, believed that allowing more maternity leave for women may seem like a move to greater equality for women but is a way of ensuring women remain in a subordinate role to men. Women are restrained by the caring and nurturing role or the housewife role to a position from which men benefit from the unpaid labour of women. By giving women more maternity leave it reinforces the idea that women are inferior and should provide free services to men through their expressive role. The New Right disagree with this view and point to the fact that women actively choose to be housewives and mothers because they are best suited to this role, as it is a biologically

determined role. For Duncombe and Marsden women actually perform a triple shift of housework, paid work and emotion work, which is caring for the sick or giving emotional support to the family.

Austerity measures have had the biggest impact on women. The item points out that women have to care for elderly relatives. Women's free labour contributes towards the economy of the male-dominated traditional nuclear family and allows men to hold on to better paid jobs and enjoy the benefits of women's unpaid domestic labour. Not only this, but they also act as role models for daughters who are socialised to the caring role in the family and expected to carry a dual burden or triple shift. Not all feminists agree with this viewpoint. Liberal feminists argue that progress has been made in the position of women because of government social policies that directly support men having paternity leave to care for children in their role as the new man. Indirectly education policies have allowed women to choose education and careers over starting families.

Two clear points are developed in detail from the item. This response shows clearly how to add detail and depth to the response and shows good knowledge of how social policies ensure the patriarchal ideology is supported.

Item B
Marxist sociologists argue that families 'mask' social tensions created by conflict between classes in society. Children learn to be obedient to their superiors so they will know how to follow orders.

Other perspectives of the family present society as based on a general agreement between all members who share the same values.

Question 12 (AS and A Level style): Applying material from Item B and your knowledge, evaluate the Marxist view of the family. (20 marks)

Top Mark Response:
The Marxist view of the family is based on the key idea that the family, like all other institutions, socialises the family members so that they do not challenge

the inequalities that exist because of capitalism. Capitalism exists because of the exploitation of a group, called the proletariat or workers, within society who have to sell their labour value to the bourgeoisie, who own the means of production – factories or land. The nuclear family is said to reproduce the ideology of capitalism, as it socialises the members to the values of the parents who are already being exploited in the workplace by bosses. Functionalists would disagree with this view as in the advanced economies of the world capitalism has raised living standards for families across the social classes.

> The response immediately discusses the Marxist view of the family in some depth and detail and with a clear understanding. There is some useful evaluation of the view that ends the first paragraph.

Marxists also insist that the monogamous nuclear family keeps wealth in the hands of a small ruling class. Engels wrote that women were given economic security for their agreement to give men legitimate heirs who would inherit the wealth of the family. The criticism of this view is that there is a diversity of family types, not just monogamous nuclear families, which exist within the capitalist economy. The nuclear family is celebrated as the ideal unit for social stability. This is a 'rose-tinted' view of the nuclear family according to Marxists. The family absorbs much of the anger that arises from individuals' dissatisfaction with the exploitative workplace. Thus the family has a dark side where the wife absorbs complaints about work. Radical feminists agree with this view and are against the patriarchal nature of the nuclear family. Marxists argue that the family acts as a warm bath easing discontents brought about by an unequal and unfair economic system. Functionalists would agree that the family acts as a warm bath. For Parsons it stabilised adult personalities, providing comfort and 'a haven in a heartless world'. Parents are more motivated to contribute to society when they have a family and so the family is not merely exploiting members,

as Marxists would argue, but also benefiting each member and so wider society.

> Excellent depth of detail in this paragraph with a detailed evaluation of the 'warm bath theory' to build on Marxist criticisms of the family as 'masking' wider conflicts in society, such as inequality.

According to Eli Zaretsky the family provides important ideological functions for the capitalist economic system as part of the ideological state apparatus. Both points so far contribute to the world view that nothing needs to change; it is natural to have male bosses with the workers' best interests at heart as it is to have a family with a patriarchal head of the household. Also the family is a safe haven for workers. Of course functionalists and the New Right would argue the importance of biological determinism in the father being the breadwinner and mother being the homemaker. Marxists go further with their arguments about the nuclear family being supportive of capitalism in that it encourages consumerism so that there is a market for the goods produced by the exploitative modes of production to enrich the bourgeois class. The proletariat are encouraged to be greedy and compete for goods so the market for 'useless' commodities is a growing one. Of course, many would point to how these goods have improved lives and sociologists have argued that these commodities have led to the 'death of the housewife' role. This means that laborious domestic tasks do not exist because of washing machines, cooking equipment and dishwashers.

> Here the evaluations appear as immediate responses to points of criticism. This is excellent analysis. Note how in the last part of the paragraph points from other topics are used in the evaluation.

The family is not only a place where obedience is learnt but also where the next generation of workers are raised for 'free'. Margaret Benston, a Marxist-feminist, described how the family maintains the healthy workforce with no cost to the bourgeoisie.

Emotional wellbeing and physical fitness of the men are maintained by women's domestic labour and sexual services. Functionalists and indeed many liberal feminists would disagree and point to the active choices that women can now make to not be part of nuclear families, yet they still choose these relationships as they too benefit from them. Marxists would argue that people are sold an idealised 'story' of what the nuclear family is like by the media.

> This paragraph develops earlier points adding the necessary depth and detail of top-level responses. Again there is accurate evaluation. It is important to provide this balance of advantage versus disadvantage to achieve the highest marks.

The main purpose of the nuclear family is to ensure the capitalist economic system is maintained. The family masks inequality between an elite social class and the workers. It also uses women to socialise and care for the next generation of workers and the present workforce. These same workers are socialised to be consumers and compete to maintain homes with the latest gadgets which helps the ruling elite to make profits. Marxism does try to explain all the problems using an economic evaluation of the family. However, if economics is so important the Marxist analysis must take more account of why people still choose these types of relationships. Not just that, but Marxists have to look at the real improvements in conditions of many workers in capitalist countries. There are many useful points made in the Marxist analysis especially in examining the patriarchal nature of the nuclear family.

> This conclusion summarises the points in the previous paragraphs. Try not to add in any new points of evaluation here. Point out the main weaknesses and try to finish with a definitive advantage that the Marxist view contributes.

Quick Test Answers

DAY 1

The Functionalist and New Right Perspectives on Education
QUICK TEST (Page 6)
1. Society works like a human body, with interdependent parts.
2. Social solidarity.
3. Schools compete against each other in a free market for parents to select them for their children.
4. Role allocation.
5. A system which allows everyone an equal chance of success based on their own ability and efforts.
6. Ofsted reports, league tables.
7. Human capital.
8. Achieved status.
9. State involvement.
10. Talcott Parsons.

The Marxist Perspective on Education
QUICK TEST (Page 10)
1. The means of production (factories, land, etc.).
2. Myth of meritocracy.
3. School and the workplace are alike.
4. Hierarchy/competition and division/lack of control/extrinsic rewards.
5. Anti-school subculture.
6. Marketisation.
7. Obedience.
8. Ideological state apparatus.
9. Reproduces and legitimates class inequality.
10. Nothing except their own ability to work.

Social Class Differences in Achievement: External Factors
QUICK TEST (Page 14)
1. Parental income and eligibility for free school meals.
2. Skills and attitudes shared by the middle class that put them at an advantage in the education system.
3. Material deprivation.
4. Halsey (1980).
5. Elaborated speech code; this is the same code used by teachers, exam papers and textbooks.
6. Fatalistic attitude.
7. Working class students wanting rewards now, rather than waiting to the end of the education system to be rewarded with significant qualifications.
8. Economic capital.
9. 33·1% (as compared with 60·9% of other students).
10. It may cause a lack of concentration in class, or health issues which can lead to absence from school.

Social Class Differences in Achievement: Internal Factors
QUICK TEST (Page 18)
1. Howard Becker.
2. Differentiation.
3. When working class students affiliate themselves with a brand in order to gain their own status.
4. Habitus.
5. Lose themselves.
6. Self-fulfilling prophecy.
7. Symbolic capital.
8. Rosenthal and Jacobson.
9. Truancy, rejecting school values and rules, conflict with teachers.
10. Rejecting accents, clothing, hobbies and interests.

DAY 2

Gender Differences in Achievement: External Factors
QUICK TEST (Page 22)
1. Sex Discrimination Act 1975 and Equal Pay Act 1970.
2. Divorce and lone-parent households headed by working 'mum' provided female role models. These two patterns also encouraged greater independence or non-reliance on the male breadwinner (as he was absent from these households).
3. Angela McRobbie.
4. Independent, career minded individuals replacing the ideas of self-sacrifice.
5. The dramatic change in attitudes toward careers and work experienced by young women.
6. Their unrealistic career plans that required no academic success.
7. Status. They could not attain status through the low paid jobs that exist for them.
8. Boys are not expected to sit quietly and rather than read they are encouraged to do things.
9. It is not macho; it is feminine and not a masculine characteristic.
10. More motivated and hardworking than boys.

Gender Differences in Achievement: Internal Factors
QUICK TEST (Page 26)
1. Stanworth and Spender.
2. That they are still authoritarian, hierarchical and patriarchal and sexist.
3. Interrupted and broke rules often, talked out of turn.
4. The way that boys were assessed changed and so it appeared that they were doing worse than girls.
5. These are usually boys who good schools will not enrol as they bring their performance in the league table down.
6. The tasks or areas of concern regarded by boys and girls as specifically relevant to their gender identities.
7. By adopting hyper-sexualised identities.
8. By shaming them, labelling them 'tramp' or 'slut' or 'boffin' for example.
9. Home life is very different from school life, expectations differ greatly and adjustments are greater for working class children whose home culture may be very different to that of the school and so it clashes.
10. Students are exerting peer pressure on girls that break gender-role stereotypes or move outside their gender domains.

Gender and Achievement: Boys' Achievement and Social Class
QUICK TEST (Page 30)
1. Tracy McVeigh.
2. Moral panic.
3. Being seen as a 'feminine' activity.
4. Lack of employment after school in manufacturing or heavy industry undermines their notion of self as breadwinner or instrumental wage earner of the family.
5. Improves their communication skills.
6. Mothers do most of the reading in the home to their children.
7. Leadership and competitiveness.
8. Lack of male role model. Men are seen as better able to keep strict discipline.
9. Haase and Read.
10. This refers to the way that a teacher establishes their authority in a school, specifically through shouting and other masculine methods of conduct.

DAY 3

Ethnic Differences in Achievement: External Factors
QUICK TEST (Page 34)
1. Sure Start.
2. Charles Murray.
3. The belief that you have little or no impact on your own success so there is little point in trying to succeed.
4. Immediate gratification.
5. The impact of slavery.
6. Chinese pupils and those from an Indian background.
7. Material deprivation.
8. Social class.
9. By the age of 16 the students had a similar standard of English to their peers who had been born and raised in the UK.
10. Parents of Chinese students often instil a desire to achieve in their children.

Ethnic Differences in Achievement: Internal Factors
QUICK TEST (Page 38)
1. Ethnocentric curriculum.
2. Labelling.
3. Tony Sewell.
4. The innovators.
5. Marketisation policies.
6. Deterministic.
7. They had low standards of English.
8. Black role models.
9. Fuller.
10. Exclusion from school.

Educational Policy 1944–2010
QUICK TEST (Page 42)
1. Tripartite system.
2. Schools compete against each other in order for parents to select them for their children.
3. 11+
4. Ofsted inspection reports, league tables.

5. Educational Maintenance Allowance.
6. Disconnected-local choosers.
7. Schools are allocated funds based on how many students they attract.
8. Meritocratic.
9. It encouraged students from working class backgrounds to access higher education.
10. Secondary modern schools (some technical schools).

Educational Policy 2010–2016
QUICK TEST (Page 46)
1. Conservative and Liberal Democrat.
2. Private companies have become more involved in the education system; they have taken control over large areas within the system.
3. Fragmented centralisation.
4. Aim Higher.
5. Cola-isation.
6. Academies.
7. Stratification effect.
8. Marxists.
9. If they have little or no confidence in the standard of education provided by their local schools.
10. VT Group.

DAY 4

Key Research Methods in General
QUICK TEST (Page 50)
1. Positivists.
2. To gather validity.
3. When a research method is easy to repeat due to following a standardised procedure.
4. Time, finance funding source, cost and the sociologist's identity.
5. Informed consent.
6. Systematic sampling.
7. Covert research.
8. A small-scale trial run of the research method.
9. Operationalising concepts.
10. Quota sampling.

Education as a Research Context
QUICK TEST (Page 54)
1. Informed consent.
2. Due to their age.
3. Ofsted.
4. As they come from a range of age groups and have differing levels of ability.
5. The wide range of different types of school.
6. Middle class and pro-school parents.
7. Students may be difficult to find in order to take part, impacting on the representativeness of the study.
8. Members of an anti-school subculture.
9. Because of marketisation schools must promote themselves to parents and will want to show themselves positively.
10. Research that is carried out with the researcher's identity and aim known by the participants.

Experiments with Context Links to Education
QUICK TEST (Page 58)
1. Positivist sociologists.
2. They are easy to replicate due to following a standardised procedure.
3. Field experiments and laboratory experiments.
4. The self-fulfilling prophecy.
5. Hawthorne effect.
6. Comparative method.
7. The participants are not aware that they are being researched.
8. Rosenhan.
9. They are conducted in the natural environment and are usually covert.
10. Because of the nature of the laboratory only small samples can be used.

Questionnaires with Context Links to Education
QUICK TEST (Page 62)
1. Positivists.
2. In order to ensure that their questions make full sense to the respondents.
3. Face-to-face, postal or via email.
4. The questions can be simply used again in another questionnaire, even by another sociologist.
5. Those from an anti-school subculture.
6. As a result of marketisation. They are in strict competition against each other so will want to impress parents.
7. Quantitative.
8. They fail to gather valid responses as there is no flexibility or ability to probe for more detailed responses.
9. Objective.
10. Parents who are keen to voice complaints about their child's schooling.

Observation with Context Links to Education
QUICK TEST (Page 66)
1. In 'overt' observation the sociologist's identity and research aim is known to the participants. In 'covert' observation the sociologist is 'under cover'.
2. They use structured observation as it allows them to put their findings into quantitative data.
3. It allows them to experience first-hand the lifestyle and behaviours of the group they are observing.
4. Hawthorne effect.
5. Deception.
6. Only small samples can be observed.
7. When the sociologist gets too involved with the group they are observing, causing their findings to become subjective.
8. They may aim to show their teacher or school negatively.
9. Head teacher and governors.
10. Different sociologists will have differing opinions on the behaviours that they observe.

DAY 5

Interviews with Context Links to Education
QUICK TEST (Page 70)
1. Face-to-face or over the phone.
2. Rapport.

3. Open-ended questions.
4. Positivists.
5. If they see the interviewer as an authority figure.
6. They are more time consuming so smaller samples are used.
7. Structured interview.
8. Interview effect.
9. Group interviews.
10. Those within an anti-school subculture.

Secondary Sources with Context Links to Education
QUICK TEST (Page 74)
1. Secondary sources are already in existence, therefore the sociologist does not have to spend time creating them.
2. Statistics that are not included in crime statistics because they have not been reported or recorded by the police.
3. Personal documents.
4. Quantitative data.
5. It is difficult to dispute.
6. The National Curriculum.
7. Triangulation.
8. They aim to show the company in a positive way.
9. Content analysis.
10. They are merely created as a result of individual choices and interactions.

Families: Couples
QUICK TEST (Page 78)
1. Symmetrical or joint conjugal.
2. Brings stability and benefits all the members of society.
3. Many have the money to buy goods and services so unpaid domestic labour is not necessary.
4. Oakley argued that industrialisation created the housewife role; it did not exist before then.
5. Dual burden.
6. The nurturing or caring role often played by women.
7. The changed position of women, better living standards and improved homes.
8. Looking after the mental wellbeing of family members.
9. Research shows women do the majority of unpaid domestic labour.
10. Men are socialised to a gender-role script, which dictates that domestic labour is 'women's' work and something a man does not do.

Childhood
QUICK TEST (Page 82)
1. Philippe Ariès.
2. It is not a fixed or universal experience but varies according to place, culture or time.
3. The high infant mortality rate or number of deaths of children.
4. The March of Progress view.
5. Falling death rates; industrialisation; laws banning child labour; laws protecting children from adult behaviours such as smoking; compulsory education; increased wealth of families; reduced family sizes.
6. Age patriarchy.
7. Lareau found that wealthier families directed their children to activities that enhanced their opportunities socially.
8. Neil Postman.

9. Acting up or acting down.
10. Sue Palmer.

Families: Functionalist Perspective on the Family
QUICK TEST (Page 86)
1. George Peter Murdock.
2. Where society is compared to a body. If the body is to be healthy all of the vital organs must work together in a healthy way to support the body of society, so the heart may be the family keeping the blood of the body oxygenated.
3. Stabilise the sex drive, reproduce the next generation, socialise the next generation, economic provision through the division of labour.
4. Value consensus.
5. The form the family takes will fit the way that society is organised economically, e.g. nuclear families fit industrialised economies.
6. Ascribed status.
7. The family does not manufacture goods together, rather it consumes goods.
8. Stabilisation of adult personalities and socialisation of the young.
9. Evidence shows that pre-industrial families were largely nuclear not extended and that industrialisation encouraged families to use extended kin to help each other financially and emotionally.
10. The family is an important unit of consumption and the family creates a safe space for all members to relax in.

DAY 6

Families: The Marxist Perspective on the Family
QUICK TEST (Page 90)
1. To ensure the inheritance of property or the means of production (factories, land, etc.).
2. Eli Zaretsky.
3. Obedient workers and acceptance of inequality as inevitable.
4. Offers a haven where tensions can be released without judgement within a privatised family; offers a distraction through the consumption of consumer goods.
5. The family is a place where we seek satisfaction through the consumption of the goods made by the capitalist economy; without families to buy the products of capitalism the economy of capitalism would be severely damaged.
6. Improved standard of living or wealth creation, some of which trickles down.
7. Mothers or women.
8. The family or wives act as sponges that soak up male anger and aggression about their unjust exploitation from capitalism.
9. Veronica Beechey.
10. They are exploited by being members of the proletariat (owning nothing but their labour value) and because they are subjected to patriarchal control (male domination).

Families: Feminist Perspectives on the Family
QUICK TEST (Page 94)
1. Feminists argue that male power rests on disempowering women by giving them an inferior role in society with fewer rewards for more work than men get. This inequality or oppression is continued through stating the argument from biological determinism.

2. They challenge a natural order. Women's and men's roles are determined by their sex and their nature, and the family enhances the natural advantages that those roles give towards stable, successful societies.
3. Employment laws, the provision of childcare facilities and the rise of the 'new man'.
4. A set of ideas that constrain women's identity to the role of housewife and mother.
5. Boys and girls are socialised from an early age to their gender roles through toys that enforce stereotypical gender behaviour.
6. Test-tube babies, abolishing marriage, abolishing families, households (between seven and ten adults) apply for licences to raise children, all older children and adults are carers so matriarchal and patriarchal figures are eliminated.
7. The family and patriarchal ideology meant that men viewed women as their property.
8. Men and women living apart from each other (different communities, governance) so that men do not have the opportunity to exploit women.
9. Men are innately aggressive and competitive.
10. Not all women fight for the same objectives; e.g. black feminists may see the family as supportive of their battle against racism within society so would not want the family abolished.

Personal Life Views of the Family
QUICK TEST (Page 98)
1. Postmodernist and interactionist theories.
2. Friends who become thought of as family.
3. The people who are close to gay and lesbian couples: perhaps friends, ex-partners or kin thought of as their true family. This is because they know they can count on them for support.
4. Becky Tipper.
5. Unpractical because the definitions of a family are too wide.
6. Any two of social class, ethnicity, intimacy, emotion, connectedness (bonds), economics, dependency. All are structures that influence choice.
7. Anthony Giddens.
8. Patriarchy is based on control and power of men over women which can lead to domestic violence and does cause gender inequality.
9. Carol Smart.
10. Berry Mayall.

Demography
QUICK TEST (Page 102)
1. These women are of working age so more likely to have children; these women have different cultural and religious values which value the family over the individual and so do not prioritise career at the expense of having children.
2. Famine, war, religious persecution, persecution because of sexual orientation or political beliefs, unemployment or poverty.
3. Education, study, career opportunities, jobs, relatives and higher standards of living.
4. Four.
5. The number of deaths of babies in their first year of life per one thousand live births of the population per year.
6. The average numbers of children women will have during their child-bearing years.
7. Children were an economic asset in the past and contributed to the household income. Now the norm is for children to have high standards of living within our child-centred society; they cost a lot of money.

8. Can result in an increased dependency ratio with an ageing population and the consequent disadvantages that brings.
9. People living longer will mean that they occupy their homes for decades longer; thus there are fewer homes for younger families with children.
10. Older people present a unique market for goods and services. Their wealth and spending power are known as the 'grey pound' and greatly contribute to economic activity.

DAY 7
Families: Changes in the Family Over Time
QUICK TEST (Page 106)
1. Rising expectations of marriage.
2. Women.
3. The New Right.
4. Serial monogamy.
5. Couples that are Living Apart Together; they class themselves as being in a committed relationship but do not live at the same address.
6. Secularisation.
7. Negative label or societal disapproval of actions or behaviours.
8. 2·9 million.
9. Changes in laws, influence of feminism/the women's movement, financial independence of women, improved education, greater individual choice.
10. Dual-earner income household.

Families: Family Diversity
QUICK TEST (Page 110)
1. Organisational, generational and life-stage diversity.
2. The New Right resist diversity of family form as it demotivates men, leads to instability, increased poverty. The traditional nuclear family is the desired stable and beneficial type.
3. Anthony Giddens.
4. Equality and individual choice.
5. Ulrich Beck.
6. Carol Smart.
7. Patriarchal values, economic circumstances/poverty/wealth, social class.
8. Unprecedented choice, create our own identities, rapid social change, pick and mix society.
9. Unstructured interviews.
10. Instability or lack of stability or destabilised relationships/society.

Social Policy and the Family
QUICK TEST (Page 114)
1. The actions taken by governments to affect the social world.
2. A specific and narrow definition of what a family should be – with roles that are traditional and gendered, with children respecting adult authority completely.
3. Charles Murray.
4. The perverse incentive.
5. The five social evils.
6. The Child Support Agency.
7. Troubled Families Policy (2012).
8. Diana Leonard.
9. The policing of families, specifically poor families.
10. The March of Progress.

Index

Acknowledgements

The authors and publisher are grateful to the copyright holders for permission to use quoted materials and images.

Cover & P1: © stavklem / Shutterstock;

p.5 (br) l i g h t p o e t / Shutterstock; p.53 (br) Lisa F. Young / Shutterstock; p.56 (bl) sfam_photo / Shutterstock; p.61 (bc) jannoon028 / Shutterstock; p.64 (lc) Rawpixel.com / Shutterstock; p.68 (lc) Monkey Business Images / Shutterstock; p.69 (br) waldru / Shutterstock; p.96 (bl) DGLimages / Shutterstock; p.101 (lc) Yoottana Tiyaworanan / Shutterstock; p.104 (lc) Gajus / Shutterstock; p.109 (br) Monkey Business Images / Shutterstock; p.112 (lc) Ewelina Wachala / Shutterstock

Every effort has been made to trace copyright holders and obtain their permission for the use of copyright material. The author and publisher will gladly receive information enabling them to rectify any error or omission in subsequent editions. All facts are correct at time of going to press.

Published by Letts Educational

An imprint of HarperCollins*Publishers*

1 London Bridge Street

London SE1 9GF

ISBN: 9780008179700

First published 2017

10 9 8 7 6 5 4 3 2 1

© HarperCollins*Publishers* Limited 2017

British Library Cataloguing in Publication Data.
A CIP record of this book is available from the British Library.

Series Concept and Development: Emily Linnett and Katherine Wilkinson
Commissioning and Series Editor: Katherine Wilkinson
Authors: Andy Bennett and Scott Keifer
Project Manager: Rachel Allegro
Index: Lisa Footitt
Cover Design: Paul Oates
Inside Concept Design: Ian Wrigley and Paul Oates
Text design, layout and artwork: QBS Learning
Production: Natalia Rebow
Printed in Italy by Grafica Veneta SpA

MIX
Paper from responsible sources
FSC™ C007454
www.fsc.org